Ice Around Our Lips

FINLAND-SWEDISH POETRY

translated and edited by

DAVID McDUFF

BLOODAXE BOOKS

ISBN: 1 85224 011 3

First published 1989 by
Bloodaxe Books Ltd,
P.O. Box 1SN,
Newcastle upon Tyne NE99 1SN.

Bloodaxe Books Ltd acknowledges
the financial assistance of Northern Arts.

ACKNOWLEDGEMENTS
This book is published with the support of
Suomalaisen Kirjallisuuden Seura, Helsinki.
Thanks are also due to Holger Schildts Förlag
and Söderström & C:o Förlagsaktiebolag,
Helsinki, for the author photographs.
The translations of Edith Södergran are reprinted
from her *Complete Poems* (Bloodaxe Books, 1984).

Typesetting by EMS Phototypesetting, Berwick upon Tweed.

Printed in Great Britain by
Bell & Bain Limited, Glasgow, Scotland.

Contents

INTRODUCTION

The Finland-Swedish Tradition

Non-Scandinavians (and even some Scandinavians) still find it surprising to learn that a large and important part of the literature of Finland is written not in Finnish at all, but in Swedish. Until 1808, Finland was an eastern province of Sweden, and was governed from that country. Swedish, not Finnish, was the language of state and the language in which nearly all cultural, educational and intellectual activity was conducted. Finnish, although spoken by a majority of the populace, was accorded practically no recognition except as a church language. The Swedish-speaking educated classes dominated the life of the province in all respects – yet only twenty per cent of them were Swedes: the rest were Finns who had acquired a consciousness of their social superiority in terms of an alien culture.

The break with Sweden that occurred in 1808, when Finland passed into Russian hands, caused a good deal of soul-searching among the members of the Finland-Swedish* administrative and cultural élite. The relatively liberal terms of Tsar Alexander I's incorporation of Finland into the Russian Empire as a Grand Duchy meant that only a partial attempt was made at the Russification of the Finnish social, administrative and educational structures.

The way seemed to be clear for a long-overdue assertion of a specifically Finnish cultural, linguistic and national identity. This new direction received its impetus largely from the efforts of four men: Elias Lönnrot (best known as the author of the *Kalevala*), Johan Ludvig Runeberg (Finland's greatest national poet), Zachris Topelius (the poet and educator) and Johan Vilhelm Snellman (the founder of the legal, techno-logical and national principles that guide the modern Finnish state) who, following the precepts of Hegelian philosophy, set about the creation of a national Finnish culture by synthetic means, drawing together disparate folk elements. Lönnrot's *Kalevala* of 1835, with its rhythmic assertion and celebration of the Finnish language, drawing on and combining elements from

---

* The term 'Finland-Swedish' is now commonly used as a translation of the Swedish word *finlandssvensk*, and replaces the old 'Finno-Swedish'. [tr.]

mediaeval Finnish folk poetry, represented one strand of this
movement; another, important one was the large body of
national, romantic poetry created by Runeberg, which gener-
ated a pride in being Finnish. This poetry was, however,
written in Swedish, and it seemed to augur a reconciliation
between the Finnish and Swedish elements in the emergent
national psyche – yet after Runeberg, the Finland-Swedish and
Finnish literary cultures began to diverge.

The reasons for the divergence were in part politico-
linguistic: during the latter part of the nineteenth century a
struggle began between *fennomaner* ('Fennomanes' – those
who wished to assert the 'Finnish' character of Finnishness in
all things) and *svekomaner* ('Suecomanes' – those who wanted
to retain the old Swedish ways). They were also social. As Kai
Laitinen has pointed out, 'Finland Swedish literature remained
a patrician literature (*herrskapslitteratur*), created and sus-
tained by an upper class, even though several authors attemp-
ted to break with this state of affairs.'* It was, though, an upper
class which lacked many of the cultural and stylistic attributes
of its West European counterparts, being made up largely of
bourgeois-living civil servants, landowners and industrialists,
who might more reasonably be said to constitute a middle class.
In the introduction to his recently-published (1984) survey of
eighty years of Finland-Swedish literature, the essayist and
literary critic Thomas Warburton even maintains that 'Finland
as good as lacks an upper class in the international meaning of
the word.'† Nonetheless, this Finland-Swedish patrician caste
had an almost masonic grip on the country's economic and
public life. Warburton writes:

> For at least five generations the Finland-Swedish bourgeoisie
> was a tightly-knit social group, which only slowly began to break
> up during the middle decades of the twentieth century. Its
> dominant nucleus was the former corps...of functionaries and
> civil servants of all grades, landowners, industrialists and
> university-educated independent professionals; a version of it
> appeared, without significant variations, in Ostrobothnia. In
> other words, this social group was homogeneous, accustomed to
> occupying leading posts, and its members accustomed to
> privileges by reason of their social position...Such a position

---

* *Finlands moderna litteratur* (Helsingfors, 1968), p. 15.
† *Åttio år finlandssvensk litteratur* (Helsingfors, 1984), p. 13.

is inevitably accompanied by a kind of clan-feeling, a caste-consciousness, an inner solidarity and thereby in turn an interestedness in the group and its life-style, which has an isolating effect and draws a line both visible and invisible around it.‡

As Warburton shows, the isolation of the Finland-Swedish bourgeoisie is reflected in its poetry, and this sense of isolation is a theme that is present in much, though not by any means all, Finland-Swedish writing even today. It was a sense that was reinforced by the linguistic and cultural conflicts between 'Finno-Swedes' and Finns, by the strong presence of the Finnish-speaking bourgeoisie, and by the ceaseless fight against the growing Imperial Russian domination in the years immediately preceding the Bolshevik revolution, a fight to which the Swedish-speaking middle classes and peasantry rallied in full force.

It was during the 1880s that the Swedish-language poetry of Finland began to turn away from the model and inspiration of Runeberg and Topelius, with their ideals of solidarity between Finn and Swede, and became more aligned with literary developments that were taking place elsewhere in Scandinavia, notably in Denmark, Norway and Sweden. Poets like Karl August Tavaststjerna (1860-1898), Mikael Lybeck (1864-1925), and others wrote a poetry that could be said to be truly "modern", and this new Finland-Swedish poetry acquired the character of an autonomous literary movement, somewhat mindful of French Parnassianism or English fin-de-sièclism, but essentially unique – a Nordic variant of the "aesthetic" artistic tendency that held sway in the capital cities of Europe: linked to the rest of Scandinavia, yet with its sights set a good deal wider than was common in Scandinavia at that time.

Arvid Mörne and Bertel Gripenberg

The two major figures of this poetic movement, if such it may be called – it extended well into the twentieth century, right up until the years of revolution and civil war – were Arvid Mörne and Bertel Gripenberg. In the work of **Arvid Mörne** (1876-

---

‡ *Åttio år finlandssvensk litteratur*, p. 14.

1946) we may distinguish nearly all of the principal character-
istic traits of Finland-Swedish writing: a deep sense of isolation,
a preoccupation with man and nature, and the tensions
between them, and an aesthetic contemplation of cosmic
realities. Mörne was born of Finland-Swedish parents in the
heart of 'Finnish' Finland, in Kuopio, where his father was
chief customs and excise officer. When the boy was six, he was
taken to Nystad on Finland's south-west coast, where both
Swedish and Finnish were spoken, and the family remained
there for eight years while he received his education in a
Swedish school, much against the counsel of the local vicar and
several of the family's relatives, who wanted him to be
educated at a Finnish school.

Thus the growing boy witnessed at first hand the asperities of
the language conflict which was a marked feature of social and
political life in the Finland of the late nineteenth century. He
also had a good opportunity to observe the social injustice that
marred the lives of the mass of the Finnish peasantry, and
began to develop a strong civic conscience, a process reinforced
by his years of study at the University of Helsingfors.* He
became involved in radical student circles, and the poetry of his
younger years is characterised by an intense preoccupation with
the social struggle, conceived of as an elemental upheaval, and
with the songs and traditions of the Finland-Swedish people,
the coast-dwelling farmers and fishermen, workers and public
servants. It is also, however, marked by an equally intense
absorption in the moods and faces of Finnish nature, particu-
larly the wild, windswept landscape of the Nyland skerries.
There is a strong preponderance of 'Gothic' and 'Viking'
themes, after the manner of the then fashionable bard of the
1880s, Gånge Rolf (the pseudonym of V.K.E. Wichmann,
1856-1938).

Mörne continued to write poetry in this vein until the events
of 1917 and 1918, which shattered his youthful dreams of
revolution and forced him back upon himself, into a brooding
analysis of the solitary individual's consciousness. The break is
quite remarkable: although Mörne continued to take an active
interest in current events, and never lost his passionate
involvement with Finland and things Finnish (during the 1930s
he wrote poems against the growing fascist movement in

---

* The Finland-Swedish name for Helsinki, the capital of Finland.

Finland), he concentrated more and more upon the elaboration of an austerely beautiful nature poetry in which man is portrayed as a lonely, alien guest awaiting reabsorption into a cosmic night. Towards the end of his life, Mörne wrote of himself:

> Yes, I was the thistle, interpreter of angry thoughts,
> full of prickles,
> Around me the happy throng of the summer meadow
> in blue and yellow.
>
> Around me the bird chorus of the summer day
> and din of grasshoppers
> and fluttering of butterflies without solace for
> a thistle-soul!
>
> And now the whole world is empty and silent
> and the meadow bare
> and I, with some few red, defiant flowers,
> stand solitary here.

The social, artistic and cultural milieu in which Mörne established himself was the Finland-Swedish literary world of the early twentieth century. Although politically radical views were sometimes fashionable in this milieu, it was nonetheless an essentially conservative, all-male, rather stuffy environment. Writing of Hjalmar Procopé (1868–1929), a poet of lesser stature than Mörne, yet more immediately typical of his time, Warburton describes

> ...an expressive caricature by Signe Hammarsten-Jansson from the beginning of the 1920s which portrays Mikael Lybeck [another important Finland-Swedish poet of the time] and Procopé playing billiards together, and a few examples of the two contestants' exchange of ideas have traditionally belonged to the classical flora of Finland-Swedish anecdotes. Little side-glimpses of this kind – piously conserved, but nowadays forgotten – say in the greatest brevity something about an earlier generation of poets and its background that is worth retaining in one's memory. The 'solitary Swedes' of male sex and a certain social status were quite frequently surrounded by a club atmosphere of cognac, cigar-smoke and dingy leather armchairs...*

Bertel Gripenberg (1878-1947), the other major Finland-Swedish poet of the early years of the century, possessed such a

---

* Warburton, *Åttio år finlandssvensk litteratur*, p. 54.

strong and individual character that he was able in some respects to transcend these cosy but suffocating surroundings. The youngest of the group of "new" poets who dominated the Helsingfors literary scene around the turn of the century, Gripenberg was born in St Petersburg, where his father was a senior civil servant. As a child he was frail and sensitive and had, in his own words, a 'pampered' upbringing; he spent the summers in the Finnish countryside, and received his education at home until he was ten. In 1893, at the age of fifteen, he entered the Finnish cadet school in Fredrikshamn, where he was subjected to merciless bullying, and finally ran away to his mother's house in Helsingfors. He took the university entrance examination in the spring of 1898, and began by studying law. As part of his course, he had to accompany a judge as secretary to a remote area of northern Finland – the journey there, through starlit forest landscapes and snowy wastes, left an indelible mark on the poetry which he began to write at around this time, and indeed on much of his later work as well. Gripenberg's legal studies were broken off, however, when he began to suffer from a chronic eye inflammation. The enforced idleness which the attacks of this disease – iritis – brought with them was a source of considerable frustration and bitterness to Gripenberg, as he reflected on how his future prospects were being ruined – but it did mean that he tended to devote more and more time to literary activity.

In Helsingfors Gripenberg came into contact with a circle of literary men who grouped themselves around the journal *Euterpe*: they included Torsten Söderhjelm, Gunnar Castrén, Emil Zilliacus and Rolf Lagerborg. Gripenberg began to publish poems in the journal, and soon brought out his first collection *Dikter* (Poems, 1903), followed by a second, *Vida vägar* (Wide Roads, 1904), and a third, *Gallergrinden* (The Wrought Iron Gate, 1905). This early poetry was for the most part strongly marked by the influence of Swedish fin-de-sièclism, at times with a pronounced erotic flavour and always accompanied by a rather cold-nerved preoccupation with style, external appearances and "panache". The best of these pieces, such as the celebrated 'Gallergrinden' ('The Wrought Iron Gate'), point towards an art of the unsaid and the unseen. As Warburton has pointed out, this was the tendency which produced Gripenberg's finest poems, and it is the one which predominated during the years from 1908 to 1917, the high point of the poet's career.

From 1904 onwards Gripenberg worked for a time as a private tutor in the house of a landowner in Tavastland (Häme), southern Finland – in the end he made Tavastland his spiritual and temporal home, bought property there and settled down as a member of the local landowning community. In 1913, as the secretary of the foxhound division of the Finnish Kennel Club he made a visit to England and was a guest of the Kennel Club of Great Britain. In general, Gripenberg's literary production of these years reflects the life of the Finland-Swedish landowning class: country houses, hunting and shooting, a solitary delight in and proprietorial concern for the Finnish countryside.

The events of 1918 proved a watershed for Gripenberg, as they had done for Mörne. The essentially conservative Gripenberg rejoiced at the White victory that concluded the hostilities of the Finnish Civil War – but the changed order of society that followed in the post-war world was not to his liking and, like the radical Mörne, he began to withdraw into himself. Unlike Mörne, however, he started to turn out a patriotic verse which at times borders on the fascistic – a token of his support for the so-called 'Lappo' movement (an ultra-right wing nationalistic popular grouping). The Winter War of 1939-40 briefly caught Gripenberg's imagination and fired his enthusiasm, but the capitulation of 1944 came as all the more of a bitter shock. 'Finis Finlandiae – it's all up with Finland,' he wrote to a friend, predicting in the same letter 'der Untergang des Abendlandes'. Refusing to emigrate, now all he cared for was to die a dignified death.

For all its immersion in an essentially provincial artistic milieu, Gripenberg's poetry possesses an energy, brilliance and fire of its own, transcending its origins and presenting a uniquely Nordic variant of a European poetic style which, in the early years of the present century, was shared by poets as widely dispersed as Yeats, Blok and D'Annunzio. While it cannot be claimed that Gripenberg had the greatness of those poets, his is nevertheless a contribution in the same spirit.

Edith Södergran and Elmer Diktonius

The Finnish Civil War was a cruel, bloody and deeply divisive event which had the effect of cutting the country in two.

Influenced by the political forces active within Russia, the Finnish Red militia (it contained some Finland-Swedes, but was essentially a 'Finnish' organisation) represented a movement of solidarity with the nascent Soviet state, and was to all intents and purposes a Finnish workers' movement. The White forces consisted of the bulk of the Finnish peasantry and a large section of the Finland-Swedish bourgeoisie, which was just as implacably hostile to the notion of a merging with Soviet Russia as it had been to the programme of Russification organised by the Imperial Governor-general, Bobrikov. As elsewhere in Europe at this time, however, Finnish and Finland-Swedish artists and intellectuals alike became fired with enthusiasm for the idea of a revolutionary transformation of mankind, an enthusiasm which often had little connection with the realities of practical politics. **Edith Södergran** (1892-1923) presents possibly the most characteristically European manifestation of this tendency in Finland, and indeed in Scandinavia as a whole. Her thoroughly cosmopolitan background – not unusual among the European upper classes of the pre-1914 period – has been described in the introduction to my translation of her complete poetry,* along with the rest of her biography, and I will point here only to those aspects of her development and creative personality which seem to throw light on the evolution and history of twentieth-century Finland-Swedish poetry as a whole.

Although Södergran's poetry displays the poet's close familiarity with and desire to emulate the models of German expressionist and Russian futurist writing, there is much to indicate that she had read and was to some extent influenced by earlier Finland-Swedish poets. The opening poem in her *Dikter* (Poems, 1916), for example, with its image of the ring that no one crosses over, bears a striking resemblance to Hjalmar Procopé's 'Disiecta membra' of 1913:

> There is a ring drawn round our souls
> and an inviolable law that orders: no one,
> whoe'er it be, may step inside the ring.
> And no one yet has broken down that law.
> There is a ring drawn round our souls.

---

* Edith Södergran, *Complete Poems* (Bloodaxe, 1984).

In Södergran's poems we may likewise see the occasional influence of Gripenberg – cf. the latter's 'Mot alla fyra vindar' ('To All Four Winds'), with its line:

I intet land, hos ingen vill jag stanna
(In no one's land, with no one I will stay),

recalling the title of Edith Södergran's posthumous collection *Landet som icke är* (The Land That Is Not).

The influence of Mörne may also be detected in Edith Södergran's poems – in particular, Mörne's adaptations of the Swedish *visa* (ballad), with its stanzaic repetitions, seem to have made a significant impression on her, as can be seen from a poem like her 'Höstens bleka sjö' (The Pale Lake of Autumn), which clearly imitates the structure of Mörne's 'Tallarna på berget' (The Pine Trees on the Sea-rock). Likewise, Mörne's favourite image of the solitary tree finds a continuous echo in Södergran's poetry.

Södergran's break with the essentially romantic-conservative Finland-Swedish tradition as represented by Mörne, Gripenberg and Procopé is made all the more remarkable by her retention, in poems that are otherwise modernistic in structure, expression and inspiration, of such concrete allusions to that tradition. Her avant-gardism is of a truly Nordic variety, and although it is clearly related to the theory and practice of German expressionism and Russian futurism, its spiritual ambience is that of the Finnish (in particular, the Karelian) landscape, with its lakes, forests and seashores, in the same way that this is true of earlier Finland-Swedish poets.

The events of the Civil War drove Södergran into an even deeper isolation than that she had known in the pre-war years. Alone in Raivola with her mother, she nonetheless managed to stay in touch with literary life in Helsingfors. That this was so was due in no small measure to the efforts of the novelist and literary critic Hagar Olsson, Södergran's friend and helper, and to those of the young **Elmer Diktonius**, who elevated Södergran into one of the leading figureheads of 1920s Finland-Swedish modernism. Diktonius (1896-1961) began his artistic career as a student of music at a conservatoire in Helsingfors, where he studied violin and composition. Later he made a living by giving music lessons, and it was in the course of this activity that he came into contact with O. V. Kuusinen, one of the most prominent members of the Finnish Social Democratic Party. This friendship, formed when Diktonius was 19, laid the foundations of the poet's revolutionary idealism, which came into its own in literary form after he had tried to make a career as an expressionistic composer in the manner of Arnold Schoenberg and Alban Berg, but had been decisively rejected by a conservative critical establishment and public.

An important part of Edith Södergran's literary output was her aphorisms, a genre much favoured by the Swedish poet Vilhelm Ekelund (1880-1949), and which later became a characteristic feature of Finland-Swedish poetry. Diktonius began his literary career with a collection of aphorisms, *Min Dikt* (My Poetry) which showed his deep concern with the problems of artistic creation, and his desire to break with the literary norms of the past. Diktonius's first mature poems clearly show the influence of Södergran, and also of German expressionistic writing. They are, if anything, even more daring and avant-gardist than Södergran's. 'Jaguaren' (The Jaguar), one of the programmatic poems from *Hårda Sånger* (Hard Songs, 1922), opens with a section which had served as an epigraph to the collections of aphorisms just mentioned. It is the *tour de force* of an expressionistic pioneer, an artistic declaration by a creative personality that will brook no hindrance:

> Biting is necessity as long as bites give life
> Killing is holy as long as corruption stinks
> and life's ugliness must be savaged
> until beauty and wholeness can grow from its remains.

The poet's consciousness is a storm:

> I want life that wrenches up roots,
> air that makes a noise, roaring waves
> floods earthquakes volcanic eruptions,
> More red in the sky, more ragged black clouds!
> Some tall trees still stand unbowed before the wind.
> Break them off, too! – and I shall sing my song of celebration
> about the sacred terror of power.

In 1922, the year of *Hard Songs'* publication, Diktonius befriended Edith Södergran and Hagar Olsson and began to write with them in the new avant-garde literary magazine *Ultra*. But the fever-heat of his earlier poetry soon gave way to a calmer mode of expression – and his initial anarchism of outlook was eventually replaced by a rather run-of-the-mill leftism.* As a writer, however, he continued to develop in a bold and original manner – through the prose collection *Onnela*

(1925), with its fresh, clear and provocative descriptions of life in a Finnish country village and the verse-collection *Stenkol* (Coal, 1927), containing lyrics of lapidary concision and sculptedness, to the collections of the 1930s, such as *Stark men mörk* (Strong But Dark, 1930) and *Mull och Moln* (Soil and Clouds, 1934). Diktonius was perhaps unusual among Finland-Swedish poets in that specifically Finnish literary influences played an important part in his development – he was bilingual – and that some of his writings, in particular his prose works, are characterised by a blending of literary Swedish with Finnish vernacular expressions.

He also wrote poetry in Finnish – some of it original, some a free translation from Swedish. His short story collection *Medborgare i republiken Finland* (Citizens of the Republic of Finland, 1935), must be viewed as a modern classic of Finnish, not merely Finland-Swedish literature, and in general he comes closer than any of the other poets included in the present anthology to bridging the gap between the two literary cultures of Finland. The energy and vitality of his writing make it fresh and invigorating, even though the content may not always be similarly gripping. Diktonius aged suddenly and rapidly, and died earlier than he might have, of alcoholism and arteriosclerosis, at the age of sixty-five.

Gunnar Björling and Rabbe Enckell

The post-Civil War years saw the emergence of a number of Finland-Swedish avant-garde writers and poets who stood out from the rest of their Scandinavian contemporaries in being fully attuned to the artistic developments that were taking place further to the south, on the continent of Europe. 1922, the year of *Ultra*'s appearance, of Diktonius's *Hard Songs* and of Edith Södergran's last great burst of poetic creativity, was also the year in which the thirty-five year old **Gunnar Björling** published his first collection of poetry, *Vilande dag* (Resting Day). Björling was older than both Diktonius and Södergran, having been born in 1887.   His father came from a military family

---

* This change may in some measure be due to the time Diktonius spent in England (he lived in both London and Cornwall) during the 1920s, and to the influences he was exposed to there.

which had served in the Tsar's Finnish corps, and at the time of his third son's birth was an officer in the Nyland sharpshooter battalion – Gunnar Björling was born in the officers' barracks on Mariegatan, Helsingfors. When Björling was four his father resigned from military service and took a position in the Finnish Post Office, becoming postmaster of Viborg in 1895. Two years later, however, he had to leave his job, as a brain haemorrhage left one half of his body paralysed and deprived him of the power of speech. For the next seventeen years, until his death, he lived in the family home in this helpless condition, and his youngest son was deeply affected by the constant sight of his suffering.

Björling began his schooling in Viborg – then still part of Finland – and the memory of its history and surrounding countryside stayed with him for the rest of his life. In 1902 he obtained a free place at the Finnish cadet college in Fredrikshamn, which Gripenberg had earlier attended. Like Gripenberg, Björling was subjected to bullying by his schoolmates, and after a year he was transferred to a Swedish grammar school in Helsingfors, taking his university entrance examinations in 1905.

While at university, Björling became involved with a group of radical students who had as their aim the overthrow of Tsarist Russian power in Finland (during the early years of the twentieth century the Russian control of Finland had intensified under the governorship of Bobrikov), and he took part in a conspiracy to assassinate Tsar Nicholas II in Viborg, which proved abortive, since the Tsar's visit there was called off. Later, however, Björling changed his political views under the influence of his academic studies, which he pursued with great seriousness and application – in particular, he was influenced by the moral relativism of the philosopher Eduard Westermarck. During the Civil War, Björling was engaged on the side of the Whites, and was awarded the Cross of Freedom.

Björling's philosophical studies under Westermarck led him to develop an ethical view of reality which was based on the concepts of 'unboundedness' (*obegränsning*) and existential freedom. The poems, or poem-aphorisms, of *Vilande dag* demonstrate his familiarity not only with both the classical and the most modern literature of Scandinavia, Russia and Western Europe, but also with the philosophical traditions of those areas. This impression is further strengthened by his second collection, *Korset och löftet* (The Cross and the Promise, 1925).

Björling was a homosexual, at a time when homosexuality was a criminal offence in Finland. His mature poetry, from the aphoristic experiments published in the avant-garde magazine *Quosego* (1928) and the dada-inspired collection *Kiri-ra!* (1930) onwards reflects a profound solitariness and a search for liberation through poetic creativity. Many of the poems of what is possibly his finest collection, *Solgrönt* (Sungreen, 1933), show an ethical concern for language as the bearer of emotional objectivity and truth in human relationships; this concern is revealed at the simplest practical level in a restructuring of conventional syntax – predicates and genitive endings are frequently omitted when one might expect them, and the words *och* ('and') and *att* ('to') are inserted in unusual positions in order to heighten intensity and increase the general sense of 'unboundedness'. Björling's inner solitariness was reflected in his lifestyle. He spent most of his adult life in the Brunnsparken district of Helsingfors, a short distance from Marshal Gustaf Mannerheim's house, on a site overlooking the sea. One commentator has described the poet's way of life as follows:

> From 1915 onwards he lived in his brother's house at Östra Allén 9, where he had a room with a sleeping alcove and kitchenette. The walls of the room were lined with black felt and it was full of books, which lay in large piles all over the floor, making it difficult to move about. The poet kept his manuscripts in the bathtub, these included poems he had written back at the beginning of the century, and he derived constant inspiration from this vast collection. He worked at his old poems, polishing and altering them, and some of them turned up in print several decades after their initial inception. He himself regarded his collections of poetry as a unity, and he carefully composed them with this notion as a starting-point.*

Björling died on 11 July 1960 of lung cancer – he had been a heavy smoker all his life.

Björling's poetry represents a direct continuation and expansion of the modernistic idiom developed by Edith Södergran. Above all, in its élan and lack of inhibition it follows her example in asserting the 'naked' individual personality to the point where its dimensions become so enormous that it exists as a cosmic, transpersonal phenomenon, a unit in a game with infinity. Where Diktonius explodes his ego into a myriad

---

* Erik Gamby, *Allt vill jag fatta i min hand* (1974).

fragments, each of which is a separate poem, Björling, like
Södergran, makes the sustained and tensed expression of his 'I'
into one long, unbroken poetic statement, of which the
individual 'poems' are only subdivisions.

The problem of the poetic 'I' was given thorough elaboration
in the work of Björling's younger colleague on the magazine
Quosego, the poet and painter **Rabbe Enckell** (1903-1974).
Enckell was the youngest son of a professor of agricultural
economy who had conventional literary tastes. He grew up in
Helsingfors, where he attended a Swedish grammar school. In
1921 he entered the University of Helsingfors and proceeded to
study art history and literature, while at the same time taking
private lessons in painting. In 1922 he had some modernistic
poems published in *Ultra*, and in the autumn of 1923 his first
collection, *Dikter* (Poems), appeared. Shortly thereafter, in the
spring of 1924, he made his debut as a painter of cubist-inspired
landscapes and portraits. At first painting was his main interest,
and he worked prolifically, turning out a vast number of oil-
paintings and watercolours – a flood of creativity that con-
tinued throughout the 1920s and 1930s. He soon found himself
on close terms with both Björling and Diktonius and together
with his brilliantly gifted brother, the literary critic Olof
Enckell, joined them in their pursuit of the Finland-Swedish
avant-garde literary experiment, even though his own ideas
were often at variance with theirs.

From its earliest phase, Enckell's poetry shows markedly
autobiographical traits. This tendency in his writing was so
pronounced that it eventually led to an artistic crisis, which was
accompanied by a crisis, or series of crises, in his personal life.
In 1925, Enckell married Heidi Runeberg, the daughter of the
poet Runeberg's grandson, Nino. Although many of the facts
about this relationship remain unclear, it seems evident that it
was not an easy one, and that the Enckells' private life was
subject to a rather high degree of emotional instability and
marital dissension. If one bears in mind the oppressively
conservative atmosphere of Finland-Swedish society in inter-
war Helsingfors, it does not seem surprising that Enckell – like
Björling – sought to mask the conflicts of his personal
existence. Where Björling, in spite of the "openness" of his
overall poetic conception, frequently resorted to a cryptic
obscurity of utterance and a burlesque, clownlike, posturing
style, Enckell sought refuge in a maximum of literary compres-
sion and a high level of allusion, particularly to the myths of

classical antiquity and medieval Europe. In some ways, Enckell's position may be likened to that of his contemporary T. S. Eliot, who also masked the unbearable tensions of an unhappy personal life behind a complex apparatus of literary and mythological allusion. In Enckell's case, however, the masking process is more thoroughly elaborated and systematic, so that many of his poems of the 1930s and 1940s require extensive and detailed exegesis if they are to be fully comprehended (much of this work of interpretation and explication has been done by the critic Louise Ekelund in her valuable Swedish-language studies of Enckell's poetry). But it would be wrong to place too much emphasis on the obscurity and difficulty of Enckell's poetry. Among the earlier collections in particular there are, for example, nature lyrics of exquisite concision and delicacy, which only make the minimum of reference to extrinsic sources, and which an unschooled reader can enjoy without difficulty.

Towards the end of the 1930s, Enckell's marriage to Heidi Runeberg ended quite dramatically when the future novelist and psychiatrist Oscar Parland took her away from him. The collection *Valvet* (The Vault, 1937) reflects Enckell's troubled state of mind, and also the growing shadows in the outside world: there is passion and grief in the lyrics of this period, as there is, too, in the dramatic poems *Orpheus and Eurydice* (1938) and *Jocasta* (1939), both of which contain meditations on the nature of woman, who is conceived as a 'vegetative-vital life-instinct' which the poet has in some way despised and offended (the influence of 1930s depth psychology is clearly in evidence in much of this writing). This inner polemic is taken further in the dramas *Agamemnon* (1948) and *Hecuba* (1952). Perhaps the fullest and most consistently elaborated statement of Enckell's poetic and existential credo is contained in the collection *Andedräkt av koppar* (Breath of Copper, 1946), especially its long poem 'O spång av mellanord' (O Bridge of Interjections), which radiates a form of smiling, pessimistic stoicism. During the 1950s, Enckell received wide recognition for his poetry and his activity as a literary critic and theorist (he was one of the most important chroniclers of Finland-Swedish literary modernism, and compiled two major anthologies of Finland-Swedish poetry and prose respectively), and art critic. In 1954 he was made an honorary member of the Swedish Literary Society, in 1960 an honorary member of the Royal Academy of Free Arts in Sweden and in 1963 he received an honorary doctorate from the University of Helsingfors.

All this notwithstanding, the 1960s and 1970s were a difficult time for Enckell, and one during which he suffered greatly from depression. During the late 1960s and early 1970s literary modernism went out of vogue; the call among young writers was for socially-engaged, collectively oriented work. The literary magazine FBT, of which Claes Andersson was principal editor, made Enckell the subject of a left-wing campaign, accusing him of being the representative of all that was, in their view, reactionary and inward-looking in the Finland-Swedish literary tradition. Enckell did his best to counter these attacks, invoking among others the spirit of Gunnar Björling to support his contention that the artist must seek to find a third way, a purely imaginative and creative stance between the polarities of right and left. Whatever interpretation may be put on the case in retrospect, it is clear that Enckell fell foul of the literary left in Finland, just as much as Björling fell foul of the literary right.* It seems that very strong, individual artistic tempera-ments must always have a difficult time in the countries of the North, where they do not fit in with the prevailing tendencies towards group conformism, both social and ideological.

Solveig von Schoultz and Bo Carpelan

The lyrical talent of the poet, writer and dramatist **Solveig von Schoultz**, who was born some four years after Enckell, in 1907, like that of her younger colleague Bo Carpelan, presented many fewer challenges to the status quo of public taste in post-war Finland. Solveig von Schoultz is the youngest child of the artistically gifted Finland-Swedish family Segerstråle, and grew up in a domestic environment which she later described as 'my home, my castle, where the greatest virtue is to be unobtrusive – either one has it or one hasn't – and where self-expression is either forbidden or concealed.'

Thomas Warburton has written that 'from earliest childhood Solveig von Schoultz was instilled with an intense, conscienti-ous scrupulosity of Christian-moralistic origin, and this colours

---

* When the Swedish Literary Society of Finland awarded Björling its annual prize in 1947, its president of many years' standing, the novelist Eirik Hornborg, resigned in protest.

a significant part of her oeuvre.'* Warburton notes that many of von Schoultz's autobiographical prose pieces 'are much concerned with guilt, remorse and regret, and with how a child with an instinct for independence attempts to ward off the demands of morality by slipping away and keeping herself apart from others. A pronounced character-trait of Ansa [von Schoultz's semi-autobiographic, semi-fictional persona] is her experience of intense empathy: objects are personified and become the bearers of her own emotions, representatives of things that need an outlet, usually the feeling of being neglected, vulnerable or exploited.'* The conflict between dependence and the need for emancipation is an important theme in von Schoultz's prose writing, and it is evident at all stages of her literary development. She has been married for 55 years of her life – first to her first husband, Sven von Schoultz and, since 1961, to the composer Erik Bergman. She has two daughters by her first marriage. It is perhaps significant that she has not adopted her own family's name, but styles herself 'von Schoultz-Bergman', or simply 'Bergman'.

Solveig von Schoultz began to write poetry early on, but it was not until 1940 that she published her first collection, *Min timme* (My Hour). A sizeable number of the poems in her early books are written in traditional metre and rhyme; the influence of the Swedish poet Karin Boye is evident in places, but an original sensibility speaks in them. As Warburton has commented, a weakness in von Schoultz's early writing, both prose and poetry, is a tendency to want to explain too much – she is a certificated primary school teacher, and worked for many years in the 1940s, 1950s and 1960s as a 'mother-tongue teacher' (*modersmålslärare*) in the lower forms of a secondary girls' school in Helsingfors. This explicatory tendency becomes modified in her later work, though it is seldom entirely absent. As her poetic career progressed, she developed, on the other hand, a greater tautness and laconicism of diction, and her imagery became more objective, working its way through poems that are meditations on the fleeting moment, on liberating experiences, and on death. The rhymes and regular rhythms of the earlier work give way to a personally-moulded vers libre, but formal discipline is never far away: in 1959, for example, she published a suite of 31-syllable poems in the strict

---

* Warburton, *Åttio år finlandssvensk litteratur*, p. 322.

Japanese *tanka* form (*Terrassen*, The Terrace). Her most
recent poetry has been characterised by an even greater degree
of formal simplicity and economy of means, and in general she
may be said to be one of the most stylistically accomplished and
culturally sensitive poets working in the Swedish language
today.

The poetry of Solveig von Schoultz finds a natural spiritual
and stylistic counterpart in that of **Bo Carpelan**. Born in 1926,
Carpelan is a baron of the Karpelain family, one of the oldest in
Finland. He made his poetic debut in 1945 with the collection
Som en dunkel värme (Like an Obscure Warmth). This was
followed by the collections *Du mörka överlevande* (O Dark
Survivor, 1947) and *Variationer* (Variations, 1950). As War-
burton has pointed out, life in the Finland of the immediate
post-Second World War era was – as elsewhere in Europe –
sufficiently drab and spartan for the demands of a socially-
engaged poetry to seem an intolerable addition to a depressing
weight of public disorientation and uncertainty that was already
quite bad enough. In Finland, as in other parts of Scandinavia,
poets turned to the experiments in literary modernism that
were being conducted in neutral Sweden, which had remained
relatively untouched by the war.

It is paradoxical, perhaps, that the "new wave" of Swedish
poetic modernism, known as *fyrtiotalism* ('1940sism'), of which
poets like Erik Lindegren and Karl Vennberg were the
foremost representatives, would hardly have been possible
without the pioneering work done by Finland-Swedish modern-
ists such as Gunnar Björling, Rabbe Enckell and Henry
Parland during the 1920s and 1930s – these poets also
influenced pre-*fyrtiotalistar* such as Artur Lundkvist and
Gunnar Ekelöf. In one sense, then, at the outset of his poetic
career Bo Carpelan was merely continuing in the tradition of
Finland-Swedish modernism – though his early lyrics do also
show unmistakable signs of his reading of *fyrtiotalist* poets, Erik
Lindegren in particular. As time went on, however, the
idealism and obscurity began to go out of Carpelan's poetry;
from the collection *Landskapets förvandlingar* (Transforma-
tions of a Landscape, 1957) onwards, they began to be replaced
by a tendency towards reflection and meditation of a quietly
meditative type, and this was to become the hallmark of his
later work.

It would, however, be incorrect to assess Carpelan's poetic
development solely in terms of this stylistic and psycho-

emotional shift. His sensibility has at all times been a complex one – like Solveig von Schoultz, he has had a 'civil occupation', working as a librarian for most of his life – should not be allowed to divert attention from the multiplex character of his poetic persona. As early as 1952, he published an extended suite of prose poems entitled *Minus sju* (Minus Seven), in which bizarre, surreal effects mingle with a Kafkaesque parabolic-narrative style. Part of this is clowning and pastiche – but there is another, darker side to the burlesque: a concern with the difficulty of the distinction between dream and reality, and a concern with language in its capacity as a bridge between objectivity and fantasy. In some ways this moral and linguistic concern may be seen as an inheritance from Björling, to whom Carpelan has devoted a full-length critical study;[*] but Carpelan's solution to the problem of the poet's responsibility to his fellow human beings takes a form different from that evolved by Björling. Where Björling pins everything on the articulation, however fragmentary and gnomic, of the total man, the authentic individual, Carpelan aims at a linguistic objectivity of a more pictorial kind (though the dimension of music is seldom absent from the work of this impressionistically-inspired poet).

A sequence like *Gården* (The Back Court, 1969) presents a kaleidoscopic but essentially realistic description of the life of a community, in a way which suggests an affinity with the techniques of drama or prose narrative, rather than those of a strictly lyrical form of utterance. *Gården* presents the opposite pole to cycles like *Minus sju* and *Jag minns att jag drömde* (I Remember I Dreamed, 1982) – yet the basic impulse in them all is the same: a striving beyond the confines of the individual lyric in the direction of a Björlingian 'Neue Sachlichkeit' of memory, emotion and imagination. In spite of these frequent experiments, however, Carpelan has continued to write lyrical poetry which, in its apostrophising of rest, coolness and things that happen slowly, has given rise to the epithet 'Carpelanian'. Although he has also worked as an essayist, novelist and dramatist, Carpelan insists, like Solveig von Schoultz, that poetry is his 'true homeland'.

---

[*] *Studier i Gunnar Björlings diktning 1922-1933* (Helsingfors, 1960). The publication represents the text of Carpelan's doctoral dissertation for the University of Helsingfors.

Claes Andersson and Gösta Ågren

Turning, finally, to the post-war generation of Finland-Swedish poets, we find that it is essentially dominated by a split between metropolitan Helsingfors and provincial Finland-Sweden, in particular Ostrobothnia – the west-coast Swedish-speaking region that encompasses the towns of Kristinestad, Vasa, Nykarleby, Jakobstad and Karleby. The leading representative of the metropolitan school of poets is **Claes Andersson** (born 1937), who first came to prominence as the editor, during the years 1965-1968, of the literary magazine FBT, which set its sights against literary modernism, considering it to be at least in part responsible for social apathy among writers and among the public at large.

As we have seen, Andersson was at the head of the attack on aesthetically-oriented literature, an attack conducted by an assorted group of writers who drew their inspiration variously from left-wing politics, feminism, anti-imperialism and children's culture – the 'pure' poetry of a Rabbe Enckell seemed to them out of key with the demands of the time, and they demanded a 'more impure' poetry, 'as experimental and ramified as possible', and open to society and its tensions. In the development of Andersson's work we can see this 'open' trend at its most innovative: from the disparate influences of American beat poetry, Tadeusz Różewicz, R. D. Laing, and his own practical experience as a social psychiatrist, he has built up a body of poetry that is wholly original, laconic, self-critical and socially aware. There is a strong vein of humour in his work – yet its concerns are ultimately serious and cosmic.

Although he has made a radical critique of modernism, one feels that Andersson has nevertheless learned a great deal from modernist theory and practice, and that this has prevented his work from settling into conventional or predictable patterns. In his most recent collections he has concentrated to a marked extent on the dialectics of interpersonal relationships, speaking less with a poetic voice than with a set of such voices, each closely attuned to a precise level of consciousness. Andersson is also a prose-writer and dramatist, and these aspects of his work seem to be making progressively greater inroads on his activity as a poet.

Andersson, like most of the poets so far discussed, has lived and worked in southern Finland, an area which is dominated by the Finnish language. His literary activity, like theirs, must in

part be viewed as an attempt to bridge the gap between the
minority Swedish-language culture and the national conscious-
ness and designs of the Finnish-speaking majority – a Swedish
language poetry which is by no means *rikssvensk* in outlook and
inspiration, even though it may derive some of its distinguish-
ing characteristics from Swedish literature; which relies for
some if its vital force on a sense of 'Finnishness'; and which
may be considered as a Swedish-language extension of or
complement to contemporary Finnish-language poetry. That,
at any rate, is the ideal which many contemporary Finnish and
Finland-Swedish cultural theorists would like to uphold both at
home and for transmission to the outside world.

Whether such a unity does in fact exist seems rather doubtful
to the present observer: a work such as Kai Laitinen's *Finlands
moderna litteratur* (The Modern Literature of Finland, 1968),
which attempts to discuss the Finnish- and Swedish-language
literatures of Finland as one continuous movement seems
ultimately confusing to the foreign reader. The 'similarities'
pointed to by Laitinen, which are supposed to connect literary
figures from the two traditions, too often seem merely a matter
of tone or subjective pathos: the truth – always implicit in the
book, yet never explicitly stated by its author – appears to be
that the two traditions have developed along separate lines,
and that any attempt to fuse them must end by looking like a
piece of cultural engineering.

The literature of the Swedish-speaking regions of Finland
offers another perspective on this discussion of national-
cultural identity. Ostrobothnia, in particular, with its Swedish-
speaking population and links with "mainland" Sweden,
provides possibly the most incontrovertible living proof that
there exists within the national frontiers of Finland a literary
culture which, though inevitably marked by the events of
Finland's history, nonetheless remains – no less than its
Scottish or Welsh equivalents – a separate national entity,
incorporated into the Finnish nation state for the sake of
harmony, yet possessing few points of contact with the Finland
envisaged by Runeberg, Topelius (both of whom were born in
Ostrobothnia) and Snellman, or with the power-centres of
modern Helsinki.

While it may be tempting, and even partly correct, to
describe the bulk of the Ostrobothnian literary production as
"regional" writing, the Ostrobothnian literary world does
contain figures of international stature – one of these is the poet

Gösta Ågren. Ågren, who was born in 1936, comes from one of the most active Finland-Swedish literary families. His brother Leo (1928-1984) was a gifted novelist, and another of his brothers, Erik, is a productive critic and prose-writer. His sister Inga, who died a tragic early death, was a poet in the tradition of Edith Södergran. The Ågren family was a poor one, the father being a "landless farmer" in an impoverished Ostrobothnian village.

Gösta eventually moved away from this environment and attended the University of Stockholm, where he wrote a doctoral thesis on the life and work of the Swedish poet Dan Andersson. He also studied at the Swedish Film Institute in Stockholm, and made a full-length feature film, *Ballad*, based on Leo Ågren's novel of the same title.

In the spring of 1973, Gösta Ågren took the initiative in establishing the small Ostrobothnian publishing company Författarnas Andelslag (Writers' Cooperative), which subsequently published poetry, short stories, novels and documentary works by a wide variety of Ostrobothnian writers, including such names as Gurli Lindén, Lolan Björkman, Anita Wikman, Solveig Emtö, Olof Granholm, Gretel Silvander and Carita Nyström. In this way, he managed to remove some of the power from the metropolitan centre, and transferred it to a strong regional base. In polemical works such as *Hurrarna* (1974) and Ågren's own *Vår historia. En krönika om det finlandssvenska folkets öden* (Our History. A Chronicle of the Fortunes of the Finland-Swedish People, 1977), the cooperative has drawn attention to the cultural isolation and relative neglect suffered by the Finland-Swedish minority, and has added an uncomfortable stimulus to the discussion of these matters among the Finnish cultural establishment.

It is, perhaps, superfluous to note that Ågren's outlook and ideas have little in common with those of present-day Finnish intellectual and ideological orthodoxy. His far-left stance and uncompromising quasi-separatism are found embarrassing in many quarters further south and east, while the qualities of his poetry are in many ways at variance with the mainstream of contemporary Finnish and Finland-Swedish poetry. Nevertheless, he has just been given his country's most prestigious literary award, the Finlandia Prize, for his 1988 collection *Jär* (Here).

Ågren has developed an intellectually austere and laconic form of aphorism-lyric, which in its concentration and imagistic density looks both inwards to the traditions of Finland-Swedish modernism – in particular the experiments of Björling and Enckell – and outwards to contemporary English-language poetry, especially that of the Welsh poet R. S. Thomas, who has exercised a considerable influence on Ågren's poetic style. This dual inspiration is hardly a fashionable one in present-day Finland: yet Ågren has derived poems of an almost steely toughness from it, poems whose directness and level sanity of diction take them far beyond the regional context in which they were shaped and conceived.

In many ways Ågren may be seen as one of the very few still-extant inheritors of the original Finland-Swedish poetic tradition, with its metaphysical concern and internationalism of outlook. One feels that Ågren, more than Carpelan or Andersson, has assimilated that tradition into his bloodstream, so that in his writing we hear echoes not only of Mörne and Lybeck, but also of Södergran, Björling, Enckell, Parland and other poets whose reputations, during the socially-oriented 1960s and 1970s, suffered something of an eclipse. At last, in the 1980s, we see the way towards a full reclamation and comprehension of the Finland-Swedish poetic tradition, the central attitude of which was given expression by Rabbe Enckell during his polemic with the 1960s radicals. Let there be no misunderstanding here: Ågren's Marxism and commitment to the left-wing cause are not in question – yet one knows instinctively that he would endorse Enckell's impassioned plea for the artist's right to a specifically *artistic* integrity:

> Must writers appear in prisons, hospitals and places of work in the capacity of teachers, consolers and consultants? Preachers? But am I able to teach, console, give consultation or preach? . . . To communicate one's thoughts and feelings in writing in the form one is seeking and which suits one – that is what being a writer means. As for the rest, each may take up a position according to his or her ability. But on demand? I would rather be considered a reject fit only for the dustbin than appear in a role I have not chosen and am not equal to.

It will, I hope, be immediately obvious that the present anthology represents only a personal selection. Many poets who might have been included – notable examples are Mikael Lybeck, Hjalmar Procopé, Henry Parland, Eva Wichman, Evert Huldén and Lars Huldén – are not present, mainly because I was not convinced that I could make their work come over strongly enough in English translation to do it justice. (I

have omitted Tua Forsström because my translation of her
book-length sequence *The Snow Leopard* (1984) is to be
published separately.) The reader of English will, therefore,
have to take my word for it that the panoply of twentieth-
century Finland-Swedish poetry is very much wider and more
varied than I have been able to suggest.

Nonetheless, I believe that the ten poets represented here do
give us some understanding of the ways in which the Finland-
Swedish poetic tradition has developed, and provide us with a
unique insight into a body of verse which has hitherto been
largely neglected or unknown outside the countries of Finland
and Sweden. It may not be possible to claim that all of this
poetry belongs to the major currents in European literature –
much of it is a tangential, border territory, corresponding to
Finland's own precarious geopolitical location. Yet it may be
salutory to realise that such an individual and even heroic
tradition has, almost miraculously, been able to persist and
flourish in the most adverse social conditions, through civil
war, world war and cold war, and that this tradition has been
kept alive in a minority language.

I should like to express my thanks to Thomas Warburton for
his patient reading of my versions and for his many valuable
suggestions, without which the preparation of this book in its
present form would have been impossible. I am also grateful to
the Finnish Literature Centre in Helsinki, which made a
translator's stipend available to me during my work on the
typescript.

DAVID McDUFF

BERTEL GRIPENBERG

Lyric Poetry

Mosaic made from fragments of emotion –
A tiny drop of elixir, gold tear
Pressed from life's dark and obscure potion –
A whole from what true wholeness cannot near –

A cipher game played with the best jewels chosen
From language and shy dreams, light, silver-clear –
Child of the present hour and of the notion
The poet creates – words' happy, blithe fakir –

A footprint of the moment's flying glimmer,
Of music no ear ever heard, a tremor,
A mirror-image poured on glistening floods.

An arrow shot high in the sky, ashimmer,
A drop of blood poured out from veins that simmer –
Behold your essence, poetry, game of gods!

The Lattice Gate

You call a sonnet poets' vain self-esteem,
That mingles emptiness with glittered rhyming,
But locks life within narrow walls, confining,
Extinguishes the hearth-flames of the dream.

A tracework gate that ends the wanderer's road –
The sonnet; but a blossomed bough is hanging
Above the wall, and through the gate comes thronging
A far-off murmur from a far-off world.

'Thus far, no further,' softly the wind whispers.
So stop here, wanderer, by the gold gate's lattice.
You've seen enough, no more's vouchsafed to you.

Outside that portal which, never opened, rumbles,
You may give ear to muted song that trembles
With greetings from that world you'll never view.

The Nightingale

I

When pain seemed merciless and never-ending,
When torture's bed was hot and dark and tight,
Outside my window then I heard it sounding,
The nightingale's clear singing in the night.

He sang to reconcile me with night's suffering,
Cool as spring water, pure, his carillon.
And all that summer's night his notes kept filling
The shadowed white of the magnolia's crown.

Another Orpheus in the realm of shadows
He seemed to me, and magic, without likeness
He filled my balcony that roses dressed.

Away from fever's anguish and night's tortures
On cool, fresh waves, on silver planks of dreaming
I was encradled to the land of rest.

II

His singing was the summer night's fair legend
About the park's dark kingdom that was his.
He sang of silver clouds that slowly travel
In moonlit radiance through the dark blue skies.

He sang of how night's velvet moths go darting
Round the magnolia in a capricious dance,
He sang of how the thicket's scented breezes
Stir faintly in the rosebeds' crimson crowns.

He sang about the shade that heals the weary,
About the tears of dew in the narcissi
Around Artemis's white statue in the park.

O nightingale, with thanks I want to praise you,
For in your ditty welled the opium of rest's poppy
That made pain flee my sickbed in the dark.

B

The Song is Best

The song is best that never sounded
In tones, but was gloriously dreamed.
The drink is sweetest that, offered, foamed
In the goblet, but was never downed.
The word is best that was not said
But only tremblingly presaged,
And the happiness glows most brightly whose splendour
You spied in your dream in the distance.

For songs that have never been allowed to ring out
Never grow tuneless or cracked,
And the intoxicating sweetness never runs out
In drink that has not been drunk.
Around words of love that no one hears,
Around happiness that can never be won,
In eternal beauty that never dies
The dream's entire nimbus is spun.

Narcosis

How sweet it is, how sweet it is to sleep!
In dreaming's darkness distant the bells ring,
Tidings of rest so long yearned for they bring,
A gospel telling of the gift of rest.

Now each pang dies away, no torments sting,
And quiet voices, whispering and muted,
Promise the weary oblivion's paradise.
Now sorrow drowses; snapped, pain's fetter-rings.

And in the twilight nameless flowers shimmer,
In the shadow green lights of glow-worms glimmer,
On soft wings shy dreams go hovering.

On a dark island out in sleep's black flood,
So far away from life that we sense death,
Repose's bells far distant, distant ring.

Before All Winds

Before all winds my craft must fare
To distant sea and unknown land.
Let the waves write the legend of my wanderings
With light ripples in the sea-floor's sand.

That glow, of whose torments I cannot be free,
Must billow up on distant seas in flame
And, blazing, sink like the sun's disc
To rest among the clouds far at the heavens' rim.

On all the sea's waves let my craft be tossed,
Let all the winds sing in my sails,
Let every coastline greet me as a guest.

In no one's land, with no one I will stay.
I'll go on board with forehead festively adorned
And sail away when my joy's at its best.

Autumn Wind

In the fields the corn stands gathered,
And the woods glow like a brand,
From the trees the leaves are whirling
Like gold from a wastrel's hand.
I feel, when the wind is howling,
That the wastrel is myself,
And the gold all my life's minutes,
Adrift down time's flooding shelf.

In the autumn wind clouds are racing,
And the air is cold and blue.
A murmur of songs and legends
Fills the aspen's crimson hue,
A sound of wild geese surging
In the scented breeze from the north.
All space is thundering and ringing
Supreme over frosty earth.

And I am the fool and the wastrel,
Wasting the gold of the days,
And in the thickets I wander
For the sake of freedom's joys.
And in the woods I'm the hunter,
And the hunter on field and fell,
Never hardworking or faithful,
Doing some duty well.

A murmur fills trees and thickets,
Where the flames of autumn leap.
The dance of the wind and the leafage
Is like the wolves' hunt for the sheep.
And the days of life that go flying,
They are the golden leaves pressed
By a soughing frost-wind that drives them
Towards a distant rest.

And I am the fool, proud madcap
Who smiles at the days' dancing ring,
At the years that have been wasted,
And the sere garland of spring.
In the wood there is murmuring and soughing,
There the hunter's the honoured guest:
Fervent and faithful he dances
At the booming dance of death.

Why?

Why did you sing only of the moment's pleasure,
The joy of the hour, the second's radiance?
Why did you say nothing of the happiness that for long years
Most quietly, purely burns – did you forget its existence?
Why did you sing of darkness, loneliness and death,
Why did you sing the frosty destinies of the defeated?

Be silent, questioner! Brief, glowing as sparks
My moments of happiness flew by.
The words of love that soon grew silent only lied,

Brittle was the crystal of my joy, volatile the wine in it.
Mine was only the blinding illusion of dream-seconds,
The twinkling fall of shooting stars, the hurrying splendour of
    feasts.
Everyday happiness, the ordinary, warm and quiet,
Never laid its head upon my fevered brow.

The day of work is long and longer is the night of suffering,
The wingèd laughter of happiness is but a swift-spent lightning
    bolt.

Fly, My Dream

Fly, my dream, fly over frozen plains,
Fly over the dead trees of woods in winter,
Soar to the distance on star-embellished nights,
Never stop, keep soaring ever further.
Burn, my longing, like an eternal flare,
Burn in dark where all seemed snuffed out long ago.
To long perpetually is to live, to dare,
Fire that leaps till ashes veil its glow.

Understand that for one who never reached a goal,
Never rested slackly on the shore at last attained,
There is no death for the hot fire that burned,
There is no measure to his longing's blue lands.
My heart's pursued by longing after longing.
Ever anew towards an unseen coast it veers –
A poet's longing does not obey the laws of space,
The land of dreams has no frontiers.

A Deserted Manor

Snow is falling. And a dog howls.
It howls like the song of mourners.
The darkness is dense, And a wind blows,
Whining around the corners.
The big house stands in silence and dark,

A solitary lamp in burning.
And over the floor a mighty snake,
My own shadow, is turning.

The doors to locked-up chambers creak,
And black windows are gaping
Darkly at the winter night.
And shadows' fingers go shaping
Pictures that move, pictures that fly,
Pictures that smile and threaten.
It is a night with no sleep or repose,
With woes that no one can straighten.

Deserted house in deserted wilds,
Past is the splendour and feasting.
Where is your lineage of noblemen now,
And where are your proud guests resting?
They are sleeping under stone and turf,
Alone and unremembered,
And others live now near the noise of streets,
Serving and struggle-encumbered.

You are past – you are past – proud lineage,
Whose head was ever unbowing.
You are past – O bygone time, who recalls
The furrows of your ploughing?
Deserted house, you are rotting away,
Decrepit, unremembered,
On a restless night I dream alone
About that vanished splendour.

The doors to locked-up chambers creak,
In the roof there's a clatter and thunder.
Like a forgotten sentinel here
Alone and awake I wander.
A lost castle in a lost land:
Perhaps I'm its last defender,
Standing my lonely ground alone
In a land our own people surrendered.

A Solitary Ski-track

A solitary ski-track trying
To escape to the forests' deep,
A solitary ski-track winding
Away over ridge and steep,
Over marshes harried by blizzards
Where squat pines stand in sparse array –
It is my mind's thoughts stealing
Further and further away.

A frozen ski-track vanishing
In the forest's lonely rows,
A human lifetime dwindling
On paths that no one knows –
Far away they are, the answers
To the questions my heart nursed –
My wandering has been a winding
Across the snow's white crust.

A solitary ski-track ending
At a sudden precipice
Where wind-torn firs are stooping
Over the edge of the cliffs –
How coldly the stars are blinking,
How shadowed the forest looks,
How lightly the snowflakes are falling
Over the snow-covered tracks.

Fragrance of Lilacs

Fragrance of lilacs, glitter of June nights,
Of darkened gold on inlets mirror-smooth,
And love that was won in triumphs of delight
And gates thrown open on worlds far removed –
Glory of lilacs in white and violet,
And shadows' depth against late clouds' red hue –
O, happiness, that life prepared for us
Once long ago, and never will renew.

Tavastland

O land that gave me in this life
The rest that I dreamed of,
When with my heart riven to shreds
I came to you in flight,
When I came like a wild beast of the forest
Looking for a corner in which to die,
O land to which I have been faithful
Through changing snow and thaw,

How strange – although born a stranger here
I put down roots with you.
You healed the worst of my sores
With the salve of oblivion.
In the lonely years of torment
And the fire of oppressing thoughts
With fine, soft threads
You bound my heart to you.

In Norsemen's veins there runs
A drop of Tavast blood –
In my heart there burns a glow
Whose origins I did not understand.
Among voices from east and west
Which call from all directions
I hear the strange accents
Of mighty Tavast trolls.

And the trolls' song entrances and lulls
In a murmuring minor melody:
'It is land, it is ground that you need,
It is earth in which to put down roots,
It is the peace of lonely villages,
It is the calm of silent abodes,
It is the radiance of glowing clouds
On a soughing evening in late autumn.'

When my cart rolls slowly
Out along the roads empty of people,
Where the hillocks of Tavastland
Stand serried crest upon crest,
When I let myself be slowly led
Further and further from the threats of life,
Then I feel my soul is touched
However hard I struggle against it.

There a mist rises from the fields,
There's a sighing in sleeping trees
And the twining belts of the lakes
Stand gleaming in a lead-grey light –
And lulling murmurs the song
In a murmuring minor melody –
I am taken, bewitched and captured,
I cannot, I will not be free.

Against Wind, Against Rain

Against wind, against rain the hunt goes on
Across fields stretching bare.
A storm is roaring in branch and trunk
And the sharp squalls tear.
The hunter's cheeks smart in the blast,
His boots are stuck with clay –
October rain, October wind,
Nordic October day.

Against the shore lashed waves are hissing.
The sky's clouds, driving, form
A black and threatening ghost procession
Before the squalls of the storm.
The dog stands breathless before the game,
Around him rain is tumbling,
In dark the rifle's lightning flames,
But the wind drowns its thunder.

Every life is a hunter's life,
A struggle with storm and squall.
Every throat's menaced by some knife,
And Fate lies in wait for all.
Lucky who, alone, has found happiness
Out on life's acid clods,
And walks a free and unbowed man
Down the world's wide roads.

Falling Star

Three people sat out on the verandah
One velvet blue summer's night.
Each of them was sitting
In quiet, twilit thought.
And two were young and in them
Longing hotly blazed.
But the third had been a witness
To the world's long years and ways.

There breakers rolled on the shoreline
And quiet the forest stood,
Beyond the bay the horizon
Stood dark with a rim of blood.
From the firmament quietly glowing
A star fell in a curving band,
And the first raised up the goblet
That he held in his hand:

'I wish for gold and honour
Upon earth's sphere, and power!'
The second said: 'Love only
Is what I wish at this hour.'
The third raised his hand up
To bring his brow a cool breath:
'I wish for the prize I shall conquer –
Rest, oblivion and death.'

ARVID MÖRNE

A Lonely Tree

An endless plain. On it, a lonely tree.
As grim as the gale on the tundra the winds of autumn run free.
And, hard as a whistling knout with spikes in its thong,
The gusts tear the tree's crown, supple and long.

Alas, this is the only tree on this poor, wretched plain
Where the waxwings of winter can gather to feast and dine,
Where children, in days of high summer, when sun is intense
Can pluck bouquets in shade and from berries make necklaces.

Alas, this is the only tree where two chattering finches can nest,
A place of outlawed beauty – shy, murmuring, self-effaced.
And, if a man fights through the sand in his wandering from farm
        to farm
He will look at the tree benignly. It guards this place from harm.

An endless plain. On it, a lonely tree.
As grim as the gale on the tundra the winds of autumn run free.
They drag the squalls from the east and snow from the lowering
        north.
The lonely tree whimpers, it quakes on the wind-possessed
        earth.

The Pine Trees on the Sea-rock

The pine trees on the sea-rock are my lyres,
And the storm is playing on them.
Skerry and islet boom. Lost fishing boats
Steer by the pine trees and head for home.

The pine trees on the sea-rock are my beacons.
I forgot them for the sake of empty strife.
Many coasts bound me and many I saw vanish.
On this one I will live my life.

The pine trees on the sea-rock were the land's marking
Before it got a name by human grace.
They'll watch it die enfolded by the sea's arms –
The pine trees on the sea-rock and the stars in space.

Epilogue

My poet's lyre is broken.
A new one's not in store.
If still you hear a raucous cry
Of gulls, sea, skerried shore,
It is the resonance from a world,
A poem-world that's no more.

For rhythm's spirit swells alone
In breasts that can breathe free,
And sprays of rhyme against the sun
Are white-green as the sea.
But struggle in grey and ice-cold mist
Is what fate gave to me.

With enemies behind, and enemies
Before, a struggle fought
With the rabble's 'but' and the rabble's 'if'
For what the rabble ought,
A struggle in mire that chokes, but where
By the age's flag we're brought.

My lyre, like the skerry's rowan,
Loved all the winds, but best
The roaming and spraying and singing south-west.
It sounded to the melody of the sea
In the days it sounded happiest.

My poet's lyre is broken.
A new one's not in store.
I'll leave them, all my songs
Of gulls, sea, skerried shore
Inside my empty summer house,
And quietly lock the door.

My Young Beloved

My young beloved, finally we've risen
To the cliffs that look out on the sea of age,
The grey, the sad. Against this lichened edge
The long swell of my yearning's doomed to lessen.

O, don't you see: I'm autumn, treacherous,
Aiming at your heart a lance that's poisoned,
You young one, glowing, whose love's unloosened
Your maiden's breast to my inflamed caress?

O, don't you sense it, when your dress is falling
In soft white eddies at your foot,
And you, like Aphrodite, smile to suit
Some paradise's coral shore unrolling,
That I am broken at my being's root?

The Ploughman

The ploughman strides across the plain in the late autumn
        twilight.
The horse's hooves tread steady time. The work drags slowly
        onwards.
The tough, grey clay is split and cleft, the furrow's line extends
Away towards some leafless willows where the ploughed land
        ends.

Hard the gnarled fists keep their grip around the worn handle.
The plain's asleep. The marshes drowse. The reeds lie limp and
        yellow.
Over soggy banks of sedge creeps the mist like smoke.
In late autumn twilight strides the ploughman with his yoke.

The ploughman's feet, like his beast's hooves, clump on the
        twilit pathway.
Long till the spring, long till the green, long till the sound of
        birdsong.

But on cold, autumn fallow land the ploughshare's bill and knife
Are clearing in the dead, grey clay a space for green, new life.

The ploughman cannot tell his beast's toil from his own slow
       labour,
Has no lofty works to will, no lofty goal to aim for.
Yet where bowed he goes he fights the plough's laconic fight,
The earth's subjected, and a people rises towards the light.

A Boat in the Bay

A solitary boat. At the tiller, a solitary man.
And all around, the empty bay.
Far out on the horizon some lonely islands stand,
Solemnly looming. In the world, autumn holds sway.

How pitiably small seem human griefs,
The sea and sky sublimely spacious.
A solitary boat. At the tiller, a solitary man
With nothing more to win or lose.

The Immortal

The star I lived on is no more.
The sun in whose retinue
the star moved round the world
is no more.
The life I owned,
the life that was the blood's delight and agony,
is no more.

That dead star among stars,
that dead sun among sun among suns,
that dead face among faces
which was mine,
I remember no more.

But I am.

The Dying Man

The dying man,
a suffering skein of nerves,
an aching world,
immobile, dumb,
raises his soundless cry:

Happy is all that dwells outside life,
happy are the pebbles on the seashore,
happy the waves that wash the pebbles,
happy the winds that chase the waves – –
happy, happy the capricious god
who sends the winds to wander.

I
shall never be pebble, wave, wind.
I
shall never escape rebirth, pain and life.
I
am fettered to an eternal pain and an eternal life.
I
shall be thus committed:
life
to life.

The Eye in the Dream

I stood silently in space. I was dead.
In my fall through fathomless darkness
I had attained my final point: my goal.

I stood frozen in space. I was dead,
but not exempt from the compulsion
to exist
and remember my past life.

Like a hermit doing penance
in the desert night under cold stars

naming sin after sin by name,
I stood in space – somewhere – beside my goal,
conscious of an ineradicable guilt,
surveyed by an inscrutable eye.

Walk in Autumn

Autumn rides high in the leaden grey sky
wielding the lash of the storm without mercy,
and on the abandoned summer path
the wanderer meets the yellow whirlpools of the leaves.

Autumn rides high in the leaden grey sky.
The storm's lash whistles without mercy.
The wanderer views the great, dark sea
writhing in agony, boiling, heaving
avalanches of waves over drowned rocks
until the day is spent in twilight, disappears.

But in the silent night Autumn gazes
helplessly down at the sea's moonlit,
gentle swell against spume-covered shores,
while the earth's wanderer, freed,
sees his world as it really is in the unchanging
starry heaven of eternity.

The Night Is Windless

The night is windless.
   Empty, the roadway's trail.
I wanted to speak,
   But to whom, to whom?
The moonlight falls
   As in some fairytale,
As on the flowerbed
   Around your white home.

The moonlight falls.
  All the silence of space
Settles on the road
  Where my steps die away.
I wanted to speak
  Of the heart's greediness,
Its joy consumed
  And gone in a day.

I want to remember you,
  Remember, if I can.
You, whom I loved,
  Do you live in my soul?
You are far too distant.
  Here is the dead land.
Of your voice I remember
  But a lame farewell.

Perhaps it will echo still
  In my poems' words. – –
The night is windless.
  Space shines empty, alone.
I wanted to speak – –
  The weights of dead worlds
Press my heart
  To a bed of stone.

The Star

A lonely summer star, inscrutable,
Steers in the light night over the skies.
Where are we hurrying? In darkness our traces cling,
Like the long roads, the years outnumbering
The single happiness, the single spring,
The single, great adventure of our lives.

So far from us, a lonely summer star
Flares in the light firmament, and dies.

The Black Star

Your light first shone when I was born,
You gave my soul your glow's dark burn.
I saw it laid waste at every turn,
That world you bade me wander in,
You, black star.

Above earth's isle eternal hangs
The starry garland of the sky,
And lives that bud and lives that die
Absorb its gentle radiance.
Eternally with our grief alloyed,
From darkness' bosom born, you rise.
A heart's deceived, a soul destroyed,
And there in its death-dream you blaze,
My black star.

The Summer Evening

The colours, spirits of the summer evening,
The silent beings float above the bay.
And all of them exude transfigured light,
As if the sea and sky eternally were theirs.
And all of them are suddenly beckoned, one by one,
Back by their master's hand.

They are gone. Only the gentle blueness,
Which, hesitant, fled, returns again now darkened,
And lingers round the shore and round myself.
So speechless grows the deep, the heavenly vault so still,
So quiet my soul, closed up in its devotion.
What do you want, blueness, harbinger of dark?
What do you want of me, who stands at life's evening?

The Giant Clouds of the Autumn Evening

The giant clouds of the autumn evening strode by through the
        firmament,
three dismal continents
in the light of judgement day,
which slowly, mysteriously moved on black and sulphur-yellow
        coasts
and changed into Africa
and Asia with Europe in tow.
And the earth saw them progress,
laden with storms, majestically rumbling,
towards their destiny of collapsing and vanishing
without trace,
forever.

Evening on the Shore

The fir tree on the shore sees its own shadow
Wandering out across the water:

'Dark tree with coal-black crown,
Who are you?'
The beat of the waves is the only sound.
Then the sea grows quiet.
Only a solitary,
Lost breeze has any life,
Settles on the aspen, falls asleep.
Then it grows quiet in the forest.
Only a solitary cloud is seen to glide
In the expanses reaching wide,
Stop above the mountains in the north.
Then stillness grows around heavens, sea and earth.

Space darkens.
The fir tree on the shore sees its own shadow
Wander further out across the water:
'Fine tree with branches strangely dark,
Without a base of stones or earth,
Say, by what sap are your roots fed,
My tall likeness in an unknown world?
Around you inscrutable twilight hovers,

Your trunk shakes, your crown quivers.
Is your bosom, dark and drear,
Awaiting some night breeze or star?
Fine tree,
You look like me.
Who are you?'

The fir tree on the shore no longer sees its shadow,
Silent forests, silent lakes
Drowse and grow numb. All grows merely dark.
Between the treetrunks the night steals,
Reaches the shore, towers above the sea,
Hurries through space,
High in the heights and deep in the depths
Lights stars, trembling and clear as silver.

Inspiration Speaks to the Poet

Do you remember a veiled summer day,
When you prayed to fate: 'Take, O take away
Whatever you will, but to my dear one give
Love and beauty in this single life we live!'
Do you remember it? – a day of haze and mystery –
You were happy then and I was hidden away.
All that you built was soon washed clear
Piecemeal by the waves of year on year.
Do you remember that it froze, your heart's recess,
Do you remember how you lived without happiness?
Do you remember me, when rejected you sat,
Embraced by autumn on a summer night?
No one healed you – only I, only I
With a song-thrush's first timid cry!
I was life and I hid sources leaping strong,
Stronger than happiness – and my name was song.

Listen to me – a voice that lonely goes,
Carrying onward to eternal shores,
Always equally distant, equally close.
Listen, and do not ask me who I am.

The Dead Man

That day was like the others,
Grew twilit as every day grows twilit
Towards evening.

My eye saw it. My brain thought fleetingly:
Twilight is falling.
And the stars that flickered on in the dark firmament
I found again indifferently,
As unwillingly as a spoilt child,
Blinking sleepily at its kind father
And yawning as he turns page after page
In a picture book that has been opened a thousand times.

*

I should have harvested eternal joy from that day's sun!
I should have gathered eternal happiness from that evening's
        stars!
That was to be the last day of my life
And its last evening.

I am the dead man and I sleep the sleep of death
And dream the dream of death, eternal.
And nothing more is given me to dream about
Than what I gave myself in my days of wandering
Along life's road.

The Lighthouse Keeper

I live alone in my tower in the sea.
Through the years I witness the same sights,
In a steady cycle smoke, sails and hulls
Move along the sky's edge, away, away,
And clouds are born in endless variousness

And the landscapes of the clouds live before my eyes,
Yet in the end I know them all too well!
All shifts around, but what happens is the same.

Once in some old book I saw
A fine name for a lighthouse: star of the sea.
I remember it when a day of sea mist
changes imperceptibly into a night of murk
And the lighthouse throws out its white spears
To shine above the desolate pathways of the ships.
I am the keeper of a star: of course.
I tread the same way through the years
Over steep paths down from my lantern room
To the deep vault in the hard rock
Where the hollow silence of eternity reigns,
And again up to the lantern and the sea.

So I live and tend to forget with time
That the lighthouse sways like a sapling in the storm,
That the sea rolls like an avalanche in the night,
Drowning the rock, rumbling, clamouring, calling
To me, a lonely sentinel, far from land.

I am a keeper and fear nothing
Except the One who is from all eternity,
Who arches the heavens and ignites the suns,
Too far away for the brief flight of my thoughts,
And yet is always near me in the sea's thundering.

ELMER DIKTONIUS

Presentiment

A seed is sprouting in my brain,
sucking life's marrow and its flow.
My cask will have blood's hue, I know
that I will end my days insane.

My grave will bear no flowered wreath,
no Christian cross with words of light.
Wind from the north. A winter's night.
But under ice the sap will seethe.

I will walk through the rye

I will walk through the rye
that sways in the wind
with lead-heavy ears
I will lie in the grass
and stare up at the sky
that arches deep blue
with swallows that glide
I will put my ear
to the sun-warmed earth
and listen to voices
that from the soil whisper:
all's living, all's living
becoming, becoming
and you'll be what all is
when it dies:
a swaying rye-ear
a gliding swallow
a lump of soil
sobbing and whispering.
And I'll stare at the sky
and the swallows that glide
and feel I'm already
what I shall become:
a part of the whole.

The Jaguar

I

From green leaves jut forth
red muzzle
eyes that glance triangularly
speckled:
whiskers, wave-motion, clawed paws –
you're flying! Jaguar that is my heart! –
Then fly and bite and rip and savage!

Biting is necessity as long as bites give life.
Killing is holy as long as corruption stinks
and life's ugliness must be savaged
until beauty and wholeness can grow from its remains.
Thus are we, the two of us, my poem and I, one claw.
One will we are, one paw, one fang.
Together we are a machine that strikes.

We want to kill the cry of the indifferent
the compassion of the heartless
the religiosity of the sceptics
the impotence of the strong
the evil weakness of the good;
we want to give birth by killing
we want to make room
we want to see
sunspots dancing.

II

Do you think
strong paws feel no pain?
Do you think the jaguar has no heart?
O he has
father mother mate, young.
The wilderness is great
cold is the wind of autumn
in the jaguar's belly dwell
loneliness despair.

The jaguar can kiss a flower.
He has tears;
sentimentality.

III

Night.
Waterfalls murmur long.
The jaguar is asleep.
An ant is licking one of his claws.
Who is whispering:
the morning is coming
sunspots are dancing?

IV

Sunspots are dancing! –
All is numbly whirling.
In a single bound
the jaguar hurls himself over
the crests of the spruce trees –
hear the laughter of stars in his roaring! –
a lightning-volt in the air:
like an arrow deep in the earth's breast.

The Sea and the Rock

I

Questions die
problems shrivel up
interests approach zero point:
there is nothing but the sea and the rock and I
who am writing about them.

II

The sea knows:
if it wanted to
it could drown the world.

(If it blew its nose
Mont Blanc would scarcely show
more than a few inches above the pool.)
But it's good-natured
like its love-hated rock.
It allows the human mould to 'like it',
it frolics
when the spring-tide
licks the legs of weaklings
and when an impudent upstart
writes poems about it
it just sings in the night
as now

Threthias St Merryn, Cornwall, 7 September 1921

III

Fröding's nonsense
about the seawind in the pines.
The sea can't abide pines! –
nor stones, either: it wants
mouthfuls of rock;
wants greenly to see its serious eye
even though it come stealing
like grass,
cravenly bowing its head
in submission
to the salty discipline.

IV

(The rock shouted:)
I am.
I am defiance.
Send them in,
your 5-storey apartment houses of flexible steel! –
perhaps they'll stick their noses
into my navels
(the thousand caves) –
out they'll rush
with the thunder of a 12-inch calibre gun

somewhere high up
foam will dance
like white snow –
I am!

V

I don't know the names of them all
snow-anemones molluscs mussels,
some of them stared at me
out of the starch blue of the swimming pool,
others were killed by my foot on the rock
as I walked to the sea.
The sea carted its diamonds
into a cave:
fragments of glass scoured matt-clear
by the salt water (blessed bottlenecks!) –
I delighted in their radiance
and stuffed some of them into my pockets
until I got hungry
(a hint
to all treasure seekers).

VI

Never have I felt the immensity of power
as I did one stormy day on Cornwall's coast.
Not a streak of light
from the cornflower blue of the clouds
the law of gravity scarcely keeping me
on my feet
deep below me the two love-hated ones
fighting their struggle of giants.
Roaring rushing
tossing splinters of foam around it
cold green with venomous malice, the one;
stiff-leggedly defiant
with lacerated face
laughing derisively
from broken ribs, the other –
my soul howled with the struggle's sweetness
and the cliff quivered where I stood.

VII

But they can also caress each other.
Then the sea tickles the knees of the rock
as my soft writer's hands might tickle
the knees of a woman.
Strange words broken sentences sobs kisses
two lovers
in the same bed.

VIII

Vanity, sea,
empty folie de grandeur
to believe oneself something
without being you.
Hourly to produce – as I do –
poems about eternity
or Faust or 9th symphonies
or to explode
in Van Gogh orgies of colour –
brilliantly suited for insects –
until we see you until *I* saw you,
saw our powerlessness
the bankruptcy of our fragility
the ten-yard flight of our souls
above imagined abysses
(the seagulls are laughing).
Jokes we make noise we make
until we hear the murmur
of some of your
most lightly bursting bubbles;
the 'just you wait' of your nocturnal threatsong –
until we become
nothing.

IX

What was *I*?– *was* I?
Something great pressed me –
I expressed tiny
platitudes.

But I know:
to life's big-city sahara
I shall take with me
a concentrated ounce of your explosive,
power-sea.
And when my soul's tongue is drying in its palate
and all the lemons have been squeezed
it will be seen
that I have sucked at your salty breast
that I possess your foamlashing energy and fury
and I shall struggle *struggle*
to the end of my days (O
it will never come!)
like you
sea.

London

I

The memory of you:
a giant conch shell at my ear.
It sucks and murmurs.

II

I remember:
the broad alleyway
in Kensington Gardens
describing the great city
with its three lines;
a summer's night
outside Baron's Court Underground Station
where the Piccadilly Line sticks its nose
out of a black fissure in the earth.

III

I have found a pawnshop in Hammersmith
which is in agreement with me
on the subject of my typewriter.
Smiling wordlessly
I fling the precious object down on the counter
in the 100-year-old hovel
smiling wordlessly
the man gives me my 3 pounds.
He knows that I will soon be back –
I know that I will soon be back.

IV

Strawberries strawberries
buy buy!
buy souls
buy shawls buy trousers
try this wristwatch!
at one streetcorner
a mother is auctioning
her 12-year-old daughter –
at the next a spiv is whispering about 'china'
(he probably means opium).
Buy gods buy corn-patches
buy love buy murderers! –
buy this tramcar! –
buy this street this district this city –
buy Westminster Abbey! –
the price is marked on everyone's forehead
and I too know what I am worth
in this haggle-market.

V

But at the intersection of the streets
the Salvation Army man
is speaking about Jesus Christ our saviour.
A small crowd is staring dully
at his businessman's gestures,
a boy spits chewing-tobacco

at the box the man is standing on.
'Sins' 'blood' 'cross'
tumble embellished with saliva
from the pathetic prophet's throat –
the crowd is grateful for any kind of entertainment.
And when he speaks of 'deliverance'
the neighbourhood whore thinks
of all the deliveries she has experienced.

VI

At last, on the track of the mystery! –
Now I know what it is the paperboy whispers
in the ear of his customers
when the coin slips into his hand:
it's the name of the favourite
in the afternoon's next horse race!

VII

There are many
who curse you and your name –
but I bless you.
You were me: poems, hunger, love.
You taught me
that ugly faces grow beautiful
when one observes them close to.

Men

Fröding

God
gave his voice a mighty volume
and called:
give me the most beautiful song!
And from every corner
of the universe
music streamed to his throne

songs of innocence songs of praise songs of faith –
saints and martyrs all dashed off
their best,
the angel orchestra turned on its *pièces de résistance*,
there was a muddle of beauteousness
of dewdrop clarity
a most eminently heavenly
texture of euphony,
and all those present felt goosebumps
crawl up and down their spines.

But in an utterly dark niche of creation
on a little planet of uncertain rank
an insignificant worm raised
its head proudly,
pointed to its own and its equals'
festering wounds
and squeaked with its wretched mouth:
'look, your marks of destiny!' –
and cursed God and the whole of his heavenly retinue
in a coarse earthly language.
No one heard it – except God.
Wearily, with heavy hand
he tapped the rostrum
bringing the orchestra of beauty to a halt
right in the middle of its most radiant climax
and told his subordinates
to note down the lovely main theme
and put it on the shelf
together with the other music of Zion.
And he wept – but no one understood why.

Dostoyevsky

A city.
A lane.
A beggar.
A whore.
Dark.
Wet.

This scurvy-ridden mouth!
This lank hair!
This vodka-babbling voice!
Wretchedness!
Oh!

Then you come; silently.
You kiss that mouth.
You put your hand on the hair.
You go; silently.

The voice falls dumb.
The leer dies.
But I shout:
Wherefore all this?
Tomorrow it'll all be just the same!

But it's not all the same.
Your memory lives on,
your Christ-gaze,
your Christ-silence,
in all of us whom you caressed,
in all of us whom you kissed
little brother

Nietzsche

The tale of the lame man.
The tale of the man
who shuffling forwards on his crutches
climbed Mont Blanc Gaurisankar etc.
The tale of the crippled man
who after myriads
of centimetre agonies
(and they are the worst)
at the summit
kicked away his crutches
and flew
(with his crippled limbs and with
the millstones of suffering around his neck)
higher than
all pilots put together.

The tale of the man who fell
(as seen from the present standpoint
of soul-aeronautics, of course)
without being crushed
in his fall
describing a line
from pretty high to pretty low

The true tale of the supermanly man
the eagle with earth on his wings.

Arnold Schönberg

He mumbles to himself,
and gnashes his teeth:
he laughs into the distance
makes the whites of his eyes dance:
he plucks notes here and there
and thrusts them together;
he makes yum yum out of ugh ugh
and ohoho out of ah –
he – Arnold Schönberg –
the wild boar in the garden of music.

Mahler

Knife-marks of pain
at the corners of his mouth –
in profile
always in profile
his eyes hard to find.
Trombones, pizzicati,
a silver grey waistcoat –
the violins rush towards the heights
narrow shoulders acquire a giant's breadth
thin fingers
in ecstasy
scratch screaming notes to blood –
a drop on his forehead
fever-hot

fascinated eyes stare blindly –
but I cannot see them:
knife-marks of pain
quiver at the corners of his mouth.

From Pictures (*Bilder*)

The Balancing Man, by Goya

You that sit there
balancing
on the outermost edge of the earth,
turning your moonsilveroil-suffused
face towards us –
Aren't you smiling, Night, because we so suddenly
leave everything
for a while:
war, peace, love, unhappiness, money –
as friends or enemies throwing ourselves prostrate,
dreaming, mumbling
like madmen in a trance,
in order to continue the next day
in the same old rut?

Still Life, by Kandinsky

The apple is almost turning into an inkwell
and the background is almost a glass balloon.
Two lines quiver with passion
and make love in a red blot.
An X-ray photograph of a hand
and a torn-up playing card –
the Queen of Hearts! – ha! – it's she who has caused all the
        uproar!

From Flash Portraits

Bach

You play the flute in a wood.
And the wood learns the melody
and turns into an organ.
And people hear its moaning
and say: there's a storm.

Björling

God's weasel goes out hunting.
And meets beetle carrot
wig jazz.
And drops peppercorns
yum yum fox-poison.
The angels yell:
he's chewing whistlepsalms
in the gateway of life!

Södergran

Starcatcher! –
your net is glitter full
of godlike detonations
and the rustle of dead flowers.
Unborn you saw everything;
sick you cured the healthy.
No one bred poem-gnats as you did:
life-living,
bloodsucking.

Light Ugly Beautiful Dark

1

Diktonius* is the name –
but I lie like everyone else.
It's not songs that I sing
but concrete,
I have no thoughts –
my interior is an iron skeleton –
My lines are those of an explosion
my heat that of a crater –
if you seek coolness
I will give you blocks of ice,
I understand much,
know hardly anything –
but what concern is that of yours?

2

Fire blooms in me! –
no buttercup: a crater!
Cataracts of fire and waterfalls of passion.
Ash stones and coal.
Soot
dust
lava lava.

The gravel ferments
The granite comes to life
rock cracks
continents shake –
man man
god god
You:
fire blooms in me!

* *Dikt*, the first syllable of the poet's surname, means *poem* in Swedish.

3

My face weeps in the darkness –
but I know I am made of granite.
The savage floods have ground me smooth
but hard:
my soul has a strange smile.

4

No one sees
my gloomy passion's
dizzying curves of joy.
But I know that my dark arrow
will penetrate the sun's light lap
like dark lightning in brilliant day.
Then heavy-hearted weightless children will be born!

5

I slipped
and fell –
and became a human being.

God how I ran! –
like all the other rats.
That is what is called
the struggle for existence,
but is really only fear.

I am still
on the move
and am looking for the spot
where I fell
so that I may escape.

6

My rage! –
with flowers! –
Fields swoon in burning colours,
earth is out of breath
sun streams
in torrents
goes precociously straight to the point.
My frenzy
makes light breezes hover
above meadows of voluptuousness.
I shout hurrah for every embrace!
My wildness
knows no restraints.

7

I am
the pointed entrails
of the harshest defiance.
The screeching contact
with life's satin skin
does not frighten me.
I hate
the sun the moon all things
even you.
I love the sorrow of my heart
the darkness of my spirit
and my soul's despair.

8

My poems are not composed in forms,
but in human flesh.
In all flesh there are sinews, cartilage,
ugly things, ganglia.
It can be beautiful –
but cut it in pieces:
it's ugly.
I am always in pieces –
no glue will hold me together.

9

They tore off the eagle's talons and said:
look, it's limping!
They smashed its beak and said:
strike, damn you!
They put out its eyes and said:
now see!
They broke off its wings and said:
now fly!
They stuffed it into a cage and said:
some eagle!

But an eagle is still an eagle
even if it's a carcass!
Tear off its talons, smash its beak, break its wings,
put out its eyes, lock it in a thousand cages –
of such is the eagle's great harsh fate composed,
of such is the air for the eagle's great, harsh flight.

10

Far from me are all chivalrous grand airs;
I don't contend, I fight,
irregularly and wildly,
with dirty hoodlum's fists
and kicks that are not allowed.
Many do not give me
their blessing.
But I sing
as I fight.
Not the glitter-stringed harp
is my instrument,
not the pining cello
or the oboe that coos
and cackles –
but the whistle that shrieks
between raw-frozen lips.
Yet I know:
it will set the train of the era
in motion.

Memory
(Södergran)

Among dark spruce trees
a flower sprang up
miraculous.
Saw apparitions
visions ecstatically
lived through,
was lashed by suffering –
and God and raspberry worm and butterfly dust
in her
sang death and life
and the motley clothes of people.

It rose and rose
the stem ever thinner
and more transparent:
a pale thread,
star lace;
whisperings came,
spoke death
the moon.

Nothing broke.
Something hovered,
floated over –
two eyes became stars,
a tepid hand
smoothed away hunched-up passion,
loosened from the marble foot
the red satin shoe.

*

Tonight a hand brings
your satin shoe to my ear.
O murmur of god and death and life,
raspberry worm-butterfly dust
and the motley clothes of people!

EDITH SÖDERGRAN

I saw a tree...

I saw a tree that was taller than all others
and hung full of cones out of reach;
I saw a tall church with open doors
and all who came out were pale and strong
and ready to die;
I saw a woman who smiling and rouged
threw dice for her luck
and saw she had lost.

A circle was drawn around these things
that no one crosses over.

I

I am a stranger in this land
that lies deep under the pressing sea,
the sun looks in with curling beams
and the air floats between my hands.
They told me that I was born in captivity –
here is no face that is known to me.
Am I a stone someone threw to the bottom?
Am I a fruit that was too heavy for its branch?
Here I lurk at the foot of the murmuring tree,
how will I get up the slippery stems?
Up there the tottering treetops meet,
there I will sit and spy out
the smoke from my homeland's chimneys...

Vierge Moderne

I am no woman. I am a neuter.
I am a child, a page and a bold resolve,
I am a laughing stripe of a scarlet sun...

I am a net for all greedy fish,
I am a skoal to the glory of all women,
I am a step towards hazard and ruin,
I am a leap into freedom and self...
I am the whisper of blood in the ear of the man,
I am the soul's ague, the longing and refusal of the flesh,
I am an entrance sign to new paradises.
I am a flame, searching and brazen,
I am water, deep but daring up to the knee,
I am fire and water in free and loyal union...

The Stars

When night comes
I stand on the stairway and listen,
the stars are swarming in the garden
and I am standing in the dark.
Listen, a star fell with a tinkle!
Do not go out on the grass with bare feet;
my garden is full of splinters.

Wandering Clouds

Wandering clouds have fastened themselves to the mountain's
          edge,
for endless hours they stand in silence and wait:
if a chivvying wind wants to strew them over the plain
they should rise with the sun over the snow of the summits.
Wandering clouds have set themselves in the way of the sun,
the mourning pennants of everyday hang so heavily,
down in the valley life walks with dragging feet,
the sounds of a grand piano sing from open windows.
Strip upon strip is the valley's motley carpet,
firm as sugar is the heights' eternal snow...
The winter steps softly down into the valley.
The giants smile.

Luck Cat

I have a luck cat in my arms,
it spins threads of luck.
Luck cat, luck cat,
make for me three things:
make for me a golden ring,
to tell me that I am lucky;
make for me a mirror
to tell me that I am beautiful;
make for me a fan
to waft away my cumbersome thoughts.
Luck cat, luck cat,
spin for me some news of my future!

Love

My soul was a light blue dress of the sky's colour;
I left it on a rock beside the sea
and naked I came to you and resembled a woman.
And as a woman I sat at your table
and drank a bowl of wine and breathed in the scent of some
        roses.
You thought I was lovely and that I resembled someone you had
        seen in a dream,
I forgot everything, I forgot my childhood and my homeland,
I knew only that your caresses held me captive.
And smiling you took a mirror and bade me look at myself.
I saw that my shoulders were made of dust and fell apart,
I saw that my beauty was sick and had no will other than – to
        vanish.
O, hold me close in your arms so tightly that I need nothing.

Two Ways

You must give up your old way,
your way is dirty:
there men go with greedy glances
and the word "happiness" you hear from every lip
and further along the way lies the body of a woman
and the vultures are tearing it to pieces.

You have found your new way,
your way is pure:
there motherless children go playing with poppies,
there women in black go talking of sorrow
and further along the way stands a pale saint
with his foot on a dead dragon's neck.

Hell

O how wonderful is hell!
In hell no one speaks of death.
Hell is built in the bowels of the earth
and adorned with glowing flowers...
In hell no one speaks an empty word...
In hell no one has drunk and no one has slept
and no one rests and no one sits still.
In hell no one speaks, but everyone screams,
there tears are not tears and all sorrows are without strength.
In hell no one is ill and no one is tired.
Hell is immutable and eternal.

The Portrait

For my little songs,
the merrily complaining, the evening red,
the spring gave me the egg of a waterfowl.

I asked my beloved to paint my portrait on the thick shell.
He painted a young onion in brown soil –
and on the other side a round soft mound of sand.

The Princess

Every evening the princess let herself be caressed.
But the one who caresses merely stills his own hunger
and her yearning was a shy mimosa, a wide-eyed fairy-tale in the
                presence of reality.
New caresses filled her heart with bitter sweetness
and her body with ice, but her heart wanted even more.
The princess knew bodies, but she sought hearts;
she had never seen another heart besides her own.

The princess was the poorest in the whole kingdom:
she had lived too long on illusions.
She knew that her heart must die and be utterly destroyed,
for truth corrodes.
The princess did not love the red mouths, they were foreign.
The princess did not notice the drunken eyes with ice at the
                bottom.
They were all children of winter, but the princess was from the
                far south and without fickleness,
without hardness, without veils and without cunning.

Dusk

Night is coming tall in his fleecy beard,
smiling a whole smile to the half-veiled world.
Formless, gigantic, out of the dumb lilacs
grow the contours of the park in the dusk.
The pretty lilacs have sleepy ears,
they are dreaming that the sun is coming down to earth...
What can a dreamlike dusk do against all the waking thoughts
that steal by unseen...

[1916]

Revelation

Your love is darkening my star –
the moon is rising in my life.
My hand is not at home in yours.
Your hand is lust –
my hand is longing.

[1916]

The Tree in the Forest

There once grew a tree in the forest –
so beautiful and strong –
I had seen it...
It rose over the mists of the deep to the summits of the earth in
        solitary radiance.
———————————————————————————————
Now I am told that lightning has struck it...
What can one do
about thunder's destruction and lightning's bolts?
I have indeed seen this tree in the forest
and shall remember it
as long as songs keep their roots.

The Bull

Where is the bull?
My character is a red rag.
I see no blood-exploded eyes,
I hear no short, fiery breathing,
is the ring not quaking under furious hooves?
No.
The bull has no horns;
he stands at the manger
and stubbornly chews his tough hay.
Unpunished the reddest rag flutters in the wind.

Fragment

— —
— —
— — — — life's bacteria thrive on your mucous membrane.
City, you wisely arched one, you have not broken my heart:
all your people come from the steppes,
even the greyest, most silent, saddest steppes
are open to the wind.
City, you suffering one, you are as gentle as a saint,
city, you suffocating, agonising one, you have deeps
where we deep-sea fish can breath.
Petersburg, Petersburg,
from your pinnacles flutters the magic flag of my childhood.

That was the time before the deep sores, before the terrible
        scars,
before rejuvenation's bath of oblivion.
Petersburg, Petersburg,
on your pinnacles the glow of my girlhood lies
like a pink drapery, like a light overture,
like the gauze of dreams over the sleep of giants.
Petersburg, Petersburg,
rise up out of golden visions!
What I love I will gather together in words torn loose.
I scatter the violets of memory on the golden pavements of
        dreams.
— —
What is happening to me as I speak?
Do I sense rightly the approach of immeasurable tragedies?
Do my fairy-tale viaducts never rise above your roofs,
do the trains not flash by with ecstatic pennants
to Berlin – Paris – London?
Will all that I see become a measureless ash-heap?
Or are these only clouds of tiredness passing?
Is our miraculous citadel not rising up out of the sea in Helsinki?
Are not watchmen standing there with blue and red flags the
        world has never seen?
Are they not standing, leaning on their spears, spying out the sea
with the granite of destiny in their petrified features?

Or is everything merely a mirror-reflection in sleepwalker's
    eyes,
do I live in a dream on another planet?
———————————————————————————

Heaven itself wants to come down to earth.
Love nothing but infinity! is its first commandment.
Dream of nothing less than of kissing God's little finger.
———————————————————————————

Children down there, loading dung onto the carts of the rabble,
on your knees! Do penance! Do not approach the holy
    thresholds yet –

Zarathustra is waiting in there for chosen guests.

Friends, we are as low as worms in the dust.
Not one row of us will stand before the gaze of the future.
With all the past we shall plunge into Lethe.
The future is rich, what have we to give from our beggars'
    rubbish?
The future walks over us with his victor's heels.
We are not worthy that the crosses should remain on our graves.
———————————————————————————

Friends, I prophesy a feast in beauty's sign...
Where can it be if not in Engadin?
The old farms stand and look:
'From where has this beauty come to us?
From where a foreign, terrible, destroying spirit with boundless
    wings,
bringing sorrow and melancholy, farewell and death,
Beauty's restless, greedy, demanding spirit...
Destroying our gaudy flowers. Smashing the window in which
    the geraniums stand.
No idyllic paths lead any more to hundred-year homes,
the road of the demons is another, the march of the demons
is the heartless flight of the suns through space.
Eternal Fohn wind leaves not a stone intact on our roofs,
the storm will not cease upon earth...
Childbed and graves, shooting stars and lightning;
days of creation.

Has not this beauty lain dead among us for a thousand years?

Like maiden Snow-White sleeping in her glass coffin.
We have wandered over the ridge of her nose, we have trodden
        on her eyelids...
Now the mountains have risen up and begun to wander,
bearing the terrifying ball of the sun in their hands.
Our old eyes can see no more.
We cannot grumble. Praised be the hand
that hangs the wreath of the stars on our ancient mountains.
As we perish we bless you, starry night beyond understanding.
Some time there will come a purer wind over the earth.
Then the human being will step out of mountains like these,
with the eternal light of greatness on its forehead.
Then Cosmos will be revealed. The riddles will fall echoing
into Minerva's immeasurable sacrificial bowl.'

— —

People, we shall forget ourselves
and be united with Cosmos again.
We shall hear the creator's voice
sound metallic out of the breast of things.
Nothing is enough for the longing that kneels
willing to draw a world to its breast.
Stream through us: eternal winds,
honey or heaven, blessing of the all!

— —

Let those who have heard and those who have seen
come to sacrifice on holy mountains.

On Foot I Had to Cross the Solar System

On foot
I had to cross the solar system
before I found the first thread of my red dress.
I sense myself already.
Somewhere in space hangs my heart,
shaking the void, from it stream sparks
into other intemperate hearts.

Question

I need nothing but God's mercy.
I go through life in a drunken stupor.
————————————————————————————

O you strangely lightening reality — —
— — — is there an amphora
for my few drops of oil of roses?

Letters from My Sister

Letters from my sister.
What can letters say
when I see you!
Does your hair not fall lightly round you in golden waves
when you come in
to tell me of your life?
Do the hems of your dress not stiffen in ecstasy as you walk?
          The earth carries you.
————————————————————————————

Why does not everyone have eyes to see it,
why does a single hand scoop from the well of the gods?
Sister, my sister,
I have received your picture.

All the Echoes in the Forest

No, no, no cry all the echoes in the forest:
I have no sister.
I go and lift up her white silk dress
and embrace it powerlessly.
I kiss you, I lay all my suffering upon you,
you thoughtless cloth!

Do you remember her rosy limbs?
Her shoes still stand in the sunshine,
the gods warm their hands at them.
Let snow fall over my sister's remains.
Let your bitter heart drive, snowstorm, over them.
With a shiver I shall tread that spot,
as the dreadful place where beauty was buried.

The Child of God

The child of god sat with me.
The gold lyre sang out of my hands.
The child of god stares out into unending dusks.
The song circles over her head on broad wings.
What do you see in the song?
It is your own future that heaves itself
out of icy dusks,
your own bidding, calling, waiting future.

Sister, my sister...

Sister, my sister, you are only little,
but you have seen God,
blest is your brow, it shines so.
Since you saw God you have withdrawn from people.
You sat down alone among the trees
but the beck was silent for you,
the birds sang no more.
Whoever has seen God sees nothing more on earth,
he belongs at home in heaven.

From Motley Observations (1919)

The houses we actually live in are prehistoric huts in comparison with the conception of a human dwelling which we carry within us.

There is something unappetising about laying hands on one's own life.

It is so strange about the art of aphorism: the play with contrasts is as trivial as a word-play, the truths are most often unremarkable, and yet this is the costume of truth, more priceless than anything else, that is being woven.

Mild insomnia intensifies genius.

The truly declassed and outcast among men are only those who have committed a base deed.

Nietzsche's strength is not to be sought in the strength of his voice, but in the highness that streams from his greatest experience – the eternal return.

One should not ask if God exists or does not exist, one should lay one's small intelligence aside.

The prejudice against God is the hardest to overcome.

Eros Is Creating the World Anew

Eros is creating the world anew.
The soil in his hands is full of wonders.
Eros does not see men's petty squabbles,
he sees with his burning gaze
how suns and moons complete their orbits.
They are so near his pregnant soul,
what is it that his wild mind dreams?
The stars course singing along their orbits

but on Eros' forehead an eternal miracle is already dawning.
The young giant senses already the great blind saga
that he plays once more.

Instinct

My body is a mystery.
So long as this fragile thing lives
you shall feel its might.
I will save the world.
Therefore Eros' blood hurries to my lips,
and Eros' gold into my tired locks.
I need only look,
tired or downcast: the earth is mine.

Ecstasy

It is dangerous to desire when one is the powerful one,
therefore my desires stand still.
———————————————————————————
Woe, the past is dreaming,
woe, we hold the unopened bowls of tomorrow in our hands,
woe, purest of all that is pure,
woe, bliss that lifts the hammer to destroy,
woe, bliss that sleeps in the breast of tomorrow.
Pleasure that becomes pain,
bliss that one only looks at with tears in one's eyes and that dies
        away.
With tears in the corners of my eyes I pronounce the words of
        bliss over the doomed world.
Why doomed? Because you cannot hear the voices of bliss,
because you sleep like a foetus in its mother's womb.

Bliss brushed against this brow that names itself mortal,
through my lips streams the heat of a god,
all my atoms are separate and on fire...

Animal Hymn

The red sun rises
without thoughts
and is alike to all.
We rejoice at the sun like children.
There will come a day when our remains will fall apart,
it is all the same when it happens.
Now the sun shines into the inmost recesses of our hearts
filling all with absence of thought
strong as the forest, the winter and the sea.

My Childhood's Trees

My childhood's trees stand high in the grass
and shake their heads: what has become of you?
Rows of pillars stand like reproaches: you are unworthy to walk
          among us!
You are a child and ought to be able to do everything,
why are you fettered in the bonds of sickness?
You have become a human being, foreign and hateful.
When you were a child you conversed long with us,

your gaze was wise.
Now we want to tell you your life's secret:
the key to all secrets lies in the grass in the raspberry patch.
We would knock against your forehead, you sleeping one,
we would wake you, dead one, from your sleep.

[June 1922]

'There is no one who has time'

There is no one who has time in the world
other than God alone.
And therefore all flowers come to Him
and the last among ants.

The forget-me-not begs Him for a higher brilliance
in its blue eyes
and the ant begs him for greater strength
with which to grasp the straw.
And the bees beg him for a mightier victory song
among the purple roses.

And God is present in every context.
When the old woman unexpectedly met her cat by the well
and the cat his housemistress.
That was a great joy for them both
but greatest of all was that God had led them together
and wished upon them this wonderful friendship
that lasted fourteen years.

And meanwhile a redstart flew out of the rowan tree by the well
happy that God had not let it fall into the hunter's claws.
But a little worm saw in a dark dream
that the moon's sickle cut his being into two parts:
the one was nothing,
the other was all things and God Himself.

Arrival in Hades

See, here is eternity's shore,
here the stream murmurs by,
and death plays in the bushes
his same monotonous melody.

Death, why were you silent?
We have come a long way
and are hungry to hear,
we have never had a nurse
who could sing like you.

The garland that never adorned my brow
I lay silently at your feet.
You shall show me a wondrous land
where the palm trees stand tall,
and where between rows of pillars
the waves of longing go.

GUNNAR BJÖRLING

From Resting Day (1922)

A flower beckons there, a scent beckons there, enticing my
eye. A hope glimmers there.
I will climb to the rock of the sky, I will sink in the wave: a
wave-trough. I am singing tone, and the day smiles in riddles.

Like a sluice of the hurtling rivers I race in the sun: to
capture my heart; to seize hold of that light in an inkling: sun,
iridescence.
In day and intoxication I wander. I am in that strength: the
white, the white that smiles.

To my air you have come: a trembling, a vision! I know
neither you nor your name. All is what it was. But you draw
near: a daybreak, a soaring circle, your name.

So I grasp you, language of gods: confession of those fallen
silent and transport of poets. So I grasp life that soars and
exults, flits and breathes. So I grasp you, only one: day above
all!

Holy vision, so you were born, wordless tone on my
forehead! And day was a silence. And quietly in objects I lay.

A singer I wanted to be, to give the suffering day, give the
happy a longing. A singer whose song would strike hard
through the day.
And the word was nothing but sounds and light in my heart!

Most is merely silent words and lies –
to the eye of day! that moves aside.
All is silent words –
to your eye: aimlessly light and fleeting, like the silence of an
          affliction.

And all is the same dance.
And day is life, and is
death.
And all is the same dance: not to look, –
and to look: with the naked eye, to look in the eye! –
clearly –
the hidden guest.

I walk alone
down the road. A burning of sun. Is it summer,
the country?

Yellow buttercups! And nettles and burdock, in fields;
            nettles, –
burdock! Not town, and not country!
I walk alone.
Yellow buttercups light my way.
In the wood, towards the meadow: boys on a path.
Boys – the mere sound of it: wood! meadow!
Buttercup-meadow!

Edith Södergran

Prophetess: downtrodden, and in hearts
glowing!
You give the courage to go down that way where are the
            arrowshots
of clear, bright eyes,
Where there is day in which, breaking,
to be delivered –
eternal seconds!

You called out, in the grey day
blazing.
Outstretched hands –
crouching down –
nothing: endlessly, endlessly.

Baruch Spinoza

A man sat there and fought and fought. And thought raised stone on stone, until the building stood complete, the temple without rhetoric or ornament, a young man's dream: in longing manly, whole –
Heaven stood raised, a fervour of reality, and – you beneath it, and a world therein.
You were alone no more.

Alyosha Karamazov

The kiss of Christ is set above the world. And you realise: this was – was all! The power of sacrifice, a kiss. And longing of all struggles, kiss: nothing but radiant gentleness. And day, made fertile!
There was nothing but a kiss.

Words are not castles in the air, mirages. Words are not the jangling murmur, not the songs that vanity hurls past.
Words are endless silent miracles. Words are – ourselves!
Words bear a scent of longing, words bear the life that is silent.
Radiant clarity, scent-bearing silence: word that is mine.

Abracadabra!
bottle and chamberpot, thunder and bang, hah-hah-hah!
lice on your ashes, toot-toot-too!
that's the song of life!
Tears and rejoicing, abracadabra, abracadabra! –
for nothing!
All peace is in heaven
Toot-toot-too, tral-lal-la! –

A silence rests; longing
brings its flower to light.
....

From **The Cross and the Promise**

The raving mystic.
God struck me, I slapped him one back. Dead, and peaceful,
corpse-white foreheads will come crowding towards me. But I
will stamp my foot and roar day of rejoicing: oaths! I shall walk
in God's burning noctambulation. There the wind's soughing
surges in the gods.

Shamans and singers! I did not become a shaman. I lacked a
singing voice. I became a singer, a singer-
                                                            shaman!

Gethsemane.
The Master looks, and in his eye there are no visions. There
are stones in his heart. Unbowed, he stands watch over the
sleepers. When they awake it is day, and the burning night is
over.

*'The Statue of Beauty'!**

To hurry through life 'in a drunken stupor',
    'to fetch that rose' 'that never dies' –
you 'need nothing but God's mercy'.
    'When the time comes
you will give the heart from your breast.'

Our lives are automobiles and railway trains and pawn-
brokers' and banks, and coffee, cakes, sausages, broadcasting,
concerts.
Our lives are newspapers and bathrooms and lavatories, and
schools or offices. Our lives are God in military music, and
Christ in business. And great grey days of trial, and no flypaper
dangling down as a reprieve.
And great and motley we draw a tiny picture on the lantern
of heaven.

I raise romantic hands, I walk on classical feet.
I am will, not expiated.
I am weak as a cloud blown by the wind.
I bear heaven in the soiled day.

* Quotations from *The Rose Altar* in Edith Södergran's *Complete Poems*
(Bloodaxe Books, 1984), pages 130-31.

I am a little Chinaman.
Suffering is not pretty, bellowing is not sweet.
I am a little Chinaman under a wide-brimmed hat, my feet go
toddling along. I hang by my pigtail in the sky.

God's style – power of becoming: rest!
Style – keeping within one's limits. All limits change. The
narrowest, purest style:
style of the growing, and of perpetual choice!

God is all the words you are capable of saying, and one
more: the unsaid.

The cross and the promise stand timeless, two hands seeking
each other.

Does God exist? God is
                           that thing in your soul –
the crane!

God is death's
blood-red flower: life!
gentle kick, that sends
the world flying.

I belong to no one, and everyone! I have a choice, and I have
a smile. I am in the process of becoming –
nothing, and everything!
I AM.

D

Edith Södergran

1.

You stand as high as 'happiness, the new disease'. I feel your triumphant moments. I see death leering. The silent stands eternal.

2.

And you, ungraspable, you gave truth more than the others. You gave death, and burning stars.

Christ and Nietzsche and others.
Incarnations of strength: whom people do their utmost not to comprehend.

As a young man, in the obscure years of his apprenticeship, Christ beheld a holy image of Buddha. And he did not know whether to be silent, to remain where he was, or to beg.
He went gathering his Master's gifts, went the way of the cross.

Death will not liberate you – it will cut everything off.

Truth – life: process of becoming, not accomplished. Your heartbeat, completed in the moment of longing.

You had better not use fine language when you come face to face with God.

Christ believed in God. You "believe" in your own salvation.

The priest of light: white, and naked!

Pure motto:
God, and excrement!
the poles that support each other, and make: white!
the airs sing, the stones breathe.
Nothing is ugly: in the eye of God-the-Becoming!
Nothing is beautiful, only to God:
equilibrium: fire!

August Strindberg

You stood against the pack of villains, you stood on the side of life's poetry, not its fine polish. You, heckler and fighting-cock, cynic and saint, with an express ticket to heaven and hell.

I am five hundred years old, yet I don't grow old. I am five thousand five hundred years old, and I am in despair. I am a man who has stopped growing. I am a death-man alive.

From Quosego

2. My 'Neue Sachlichkeit'

Kili kili-kau!
kili kili kau-kau!
kili-kau!
kili kiliman ja-ja-ja!
kili kili kau −
ki!
kiliman kiliman kiliman kiliman −
ja!
kiliman kiliman kiliman kiliman −
ja!
ki-ka-ki! ki-li-li-li!
kili kili kili
kiliman kiliman −
ja-
ro!

58. Pigs can be recognised by the sugar around their mouths.
68. We cannot give truth to those who want to determine what it shall be like.

From **Kiri-ra!** (1930)

Jazz

1.

Today is next spring
spring, spring, spring,
hi, hey-ha-ho, ho ho ho!
what am I in this sunny part of town
with tall rose and platinum
it all goes in my mouth,
cider and milk, dear me!

2.

Screeching, drumming,
we're dancing, scampering
out into the world.
Was I born with jazz in blood and belly,
tell me, how're things dancing
for me as a millionaire?

3.

Are we going crazy?
Our tails wagging
our feet clattering
on the floor, nothing else: dancing
and not standing
embarrassed.

4.

Oh, how they laugh
market of youth
these carpets and the beat!
Who's drawn lines clear?

5.

But our tongue's bawl
is a carnival
and love's wave
falls.

6.

Twelve o'clock cha-ra cha-ri cha-ra!
ha! It's sponge-cake
music from now on
tim-tim
crash! this coloured top
cuts strips of board, violin and saxophone
clip-clap! taramtam-
tam!

7.

WHEN JAZZ IS OVER

Please please
play,
my tears are burning
my pain is blessing,
my ego's obduracy
one minute
more!

8.

It's the time when lamps glow faintly
clatter of cups and glasses
music puts on its blue jacket
the echo is heard from different tables
I have said my last step's
goodnight.

*   *   *

I am analysable
to those who have accepted.

Slowly my words are dying, like the rest of the verbiage.

We live long in the soil of others' hearts.

On us soundlights are constructed.

– that we are, that is the platform.

* * *

I am an old pecoralist,
I am not very talented,
I am perseverance and a future –
I am a new bacillus.

This morning. Calm
and the cry of gulls.
A boat and a flower
are land and water.
The flower's boat is the day's
air below the horizon.

The leafless branches rise up out of the ground,
it is bare and hard with light-flying snowdust over sand and
          rockfaces.
The colourless belt of the waves beneath the autumn trees's
          immobility.
The red light in this lifelessness;
and the sea's roaring has an even greyness.

   The microcosm of a word's line. But I remember the
unreflected long afterwards.

   The and-or-not of our motley existence!

   We all know that now, and the darkness of chaos when day
knocks us down.

Is not dada necessary for lightweightless eyes?

DADA:

> I slay dust beneath my foot,
> I am the voice shaken out into space,
> I am the sieve that let through
> and built the hall of pillars.

Your lip gives off its colour and the tongues twist, you change
your head, you meet the gaze of your fate on the streetcorner or
right in front of your very nose's cut-out.

From Sungreen

The Temptation:

Now is the hour of the sunshine's longing
and I get up on the trampolines and move to and fro
up here. Jump down, they call to me from down there.
But I know that I can't; no one can.
For no one has flown up here where no limits prevail.
I stand with my arms thrown wide, and point to my black
          birthmarks: is it not enough?
And the sunshine which has not hesitated!
Then I shall climb in fire-beautiful flame to the drowning gods of
          the darkness.

I want to live in the city as it is
with WC, electric light, gas-stove
and swept streets
a rich man's park at every other corner
and palaces and cafés, abundance spread out in windows,
and for five marks or 2 marks a rectilinear
splendour.

a sea of light and motley colours
and faces, fates
and the light of the sky – an irritant to thoughts and struggle and
        newly-ignited love
for one and one
and for all, all!
to be like a plant in a spring meadow
to stand like a tree among trees
to fill one's place like a stone among stones
in a building,
to know that thousands love and rejoice and have worries
and the same lovely eyes smile tears and burn and suffocate,
        dream, stumble, go under,
but will go towards a realm for all and a heroes' feat with light
        perspectives.
– I rejoice in the city's streets, factories,
and beauty is outside and inside.
The sky and the water stand equal
and the night is not so dark beneath streetlamps around street
        and water.
Emptiness acquires sound from the dance of the whole, from its
        cries despair and solidarity with the manifold familiar,
and it is lonely to bear one's fate amidst the gaze of thousands,
        and to struggle in their swarm
is like struggling in a tunnel beneath the burdened vault of the
        forest
with the vault of the stars concealed in one's heart.
The rumbling of cities – all!
an equal and brother to all
and the struggle against all
and finally the eyes, the many eyes
familiar,
not-so-familiar, that we carry about as in a bowl
so that they will not spill out.

The formula?
because we can't stop – because we race like bloodhounds after
        the pig we held by the tail, and devour it with its ears still
        raw.
The formula?

because we took the pigsty and sank our teeth in, pierced the
  ears of the angels and smote the devil dead, burst to
  pieces the church wall and tore in fragments the
  feather-rugs of the script of lies.
The formula?
  because we understood that all is lost,
  or nothing. In every mouthful of sausage we consume
  with our hungry tongues are opened capsules
to heaven.

In every faith that is not the golden book of despair and the
  horseman's spur of hesitation, we must be dead people,
  whom no one ever digs up.
– We must know: our happiness is as nothing, god's distortions
  are all the things that do not rush through us
like the crown of the conglomerate and the self-evident
  argument, without meaning, without answer, without
  excuse, –
like the joy of being a midge on the midges' swarming-day.
Who can tell what the midges' dance means to the midges, to us
  and the soil?
that they sing so beautifully
that it is as if the cosmos were resting on its wings?
This new belly-dance and jargon and harp-sound under the
  fingers of our hands, what is it we want to have said?
the faith that will not loosen its grip on us!
the faith that transfigures everything and demands nothing,
  since it bears – in the eternally changing – the demands
  of life.
The faith that is the pigslayer
and the master gatherer: come all ye! –
Where there are will and violence, objects rise up and eternity's
  morethanjoy
understreams; all is an aboutoneanother
on the ragfields of necessity,
the exultant breakdown of souls:
You are me, I am you
and it makes no difference how impudently false our souls are,
the same night of horror
and the same infinity bear our steps
and hide away the graves in the cheekbones of our days

so that we see drunken pigs in the heavenly firmament
and paradise and the mouth of laziness are our resting beds.
Arise, you of the honestflame: dried footsole!
sink, radiance of emptiness
on the slightest!
Go out like these tangles, there are beautyspots everywhere
and we stand still in the midst of our important doings, we wash
        out the mouths of the day-labourers
and pray: sing the glory
of the facts of life!
Sing the heaven of the hungry, you have seen more than we
        have.
We stand still before all and say:
greater than facts is the place
of the unique gleam on your glowing, hurtling way.

We are all like "mumblers" or sin-and-fire worshippers
in the pleasure
of embracing a chairleg, of tearing the ground apart and
        disappearing like mould, blood, saliva
in the facial striation of our paralysis.
A sound, physical, sense-movements' commutation, erupting
to universality and the miracle-dance of the voices
in our ears, mouths and lungs,
like a river we are, in Pentecostal tongue-talking, in the shady
        assemblies and the dervishes' dance,
in the temple of Isis
and at the jazz ball, in the passage of the orchestra through the
        eras.
There is the same raving in the pillar-saint and the Buddha-
        statues, everything is the suprasensuality
of the cross
and the pleasure-torrent
of the eternally coursing blood.
On beds of horsehair gods are nailed
as to splendour of secret delights,
like an enfeebled echo are the pitiful prayers of faith
and the most wildly clear baritone.
The same need's resplendent light and saturation of muddle is in
        every classical outline

like a mastering and a heroic feat to keep the godly limbs tensed
    together in an eternal coitus –,

or merely sentimental bourgeois incompetence,
or the interplay of all healthy instincts and tragic reality and
    voices of reason,
the reality that stands with its blue-eyed instinctual ecstasy
and the reason, sense and moderation of the unique drunken-
    ness
endless moderation, spring mountain in the eye
and sword of Damocles for all –
the mastering of the great confusion: and we know that all,
all is the probing wind of common sense
and this Eros that will not let go of anyone

and will not yield, no matter where we go.
This instinct forces all into the great sperm flood.
All is like a servant-girls' park, and is a dread
like a trembling of world instinct, primeval instinct,
of a split that wants to be joined,
and each lip that presses itself to the bread is the same as the
    copulation of two bodies.
And air and lung are the same, and each image and the eye that
    receives it.
All is a cry from rotten shreds or fresh ones
in their master's heaven, in their erosglee,
there is nothing a man will or can
or ought –
only the embrace with god!
It is that voice of greatness and the riddle
it is that murmur that explains
it is the sermon-text of expiation
in different languages, in all the forms of insanity and meanness.
The same mercy of god in all acts of recklessness and in all
    considerations.
The same power of soul is the power of fate in our days, cannon
    salute in the silence of the heart, in the sky-highness that
    never dies but sees with the courage of the clear eye,

– and day stands, though villainy, crime and rape are the sparks
      that bear lights into the darkness.
Like a splash of God's blood is each moment an object in my
      hand.
– like tufts on the skin of the ordinary we shall walk on the wrath
      that wells from our intestines.
Like a cosmopolitanism, without losing our balance
in the increasing movement. We
with the will of our hands, that our breasts might rest as in
      dissolvedness,
and all were sprays and streams
and as though all were like a well-run milkbar
in which all receive exactly as much as they can drink.
And all the eras are like a hymn to themselves,
all eras are the royal infant they raise up with milk-white limbs.
All eras are the world tranquillity that sways in their eyes,
all eras are like opened wounds, and we suffer from and for one
      another,
all eras are like the steps of dancers with inturned toes.
But there is the foal of unbounding like a smooth leap on the
      boards,
there are crazed lovers who did not need to finger their
      sordidness
there are those whose eyes can purify.

The God of the Uncompleted

It is not death's sweet bosom
it is not soft earth
and cold depths on bridges of moonbeams.
It is not the 'end with a bang' of last autumn that is forgotten for
      the life that beats in other hearts' chambers
It is not the courageous eye of liberation that escaped the
      persecutors and thought and hoped for nothing.

It is torment that cannot end, the torment of the uncompleted
the leering eyes of the living death: 'I will arrive, you do not
      know when and will not be ready

I will suck you in, you will smell my odour, the mucous wind of
      my teeth, the drive of emptiness over rattling bone pipes
the horrible thing you will not overcome – not to have brought
      order into your affairs that live on; what you have given
      rise to
I will disentangle,
with my black fingernails I will read the papers of your secret
      thoughts, the ones you did not destroy,
and I will strew the thoughts of your life's papers like dead things
      onto the roads,
do not be afraid, no one will pay any attention, whether it be a
      king's honour, a hero's legend, or merely your spirit's
      bankruptcy.
All will rise up and unravel in the emptiness of the world and the
      roses you have not won.
All that you could not manage will stand there like a confused
      jumble, the least and the greatest, you will not be able to
      pull yourself together, prepare yourself, you will not get
      a moment's rest,
I see you, I come like night's shadows out of the cupboard, rise
      up under the chairs,
I am the pillowcase and the view through the window when you
      awake.

I! remember you
I am your murdered instincts
I am your fate that lurks in wait for you
I am your happiness that stole away, I am virtue's reward, that
      took the roses from you, I am the greatest darkness that
      will not let you smile
I am the one you must overcome from day to day
I am the ruler of mankind,
in the midst of its joy I whisper with this enervated
      unpreparedness, this thing that makes you turn away.
I am the master-builder of the rich cities.
When you are not expecting me, I will have arrived.
When you are dead, we shall hold hands with each other.
When you die you will see me.

I am what lurks beneath the ships. I am surely there.
The compass is mounted in my eye
you print your sun-eyes on me.
But I shall come and devour what your longing has not been able
        to bear.
I am I, like the day of pure Meaning.'

RABBE ENCKELL

I cannot imitate
time's grey patina.
I love all that is new and inimitable.
I paint the earth
in the brilliant varnish of the spring torrent.
The sharp odour of freshly painted wood
will not quickly leave my works.

*

The sunny mass
of the Acropolis
does not frighten me.
I have seen
the Finnish knoll's
grey barn,
its temple-like
proportions
rising
weightless
towards the infinite expanse
of the spring sky.

*

The calf of one summer surveys the earth with glistening eyes.
In his great black eyeball swim the cloud and the brook's foam
and the springtime's colourless gnat flits from the green birch
          leaves
to be reflected in it
as if it were one of the forest's blind pools.

*

'Miniature Poetry'

The morning dew has placed small weights
in the dew-cup's bowl – the scales are even.
With quivering blades the lawn checks
the weight of each drop.

But the sun dips his finger in the dew so that nothing is left.
And the nettles in the ditch know full well
that the dew's weights are merely bunglers' trinkets
compared to the gigantic river in Pernambuco.

*

I am the springtime's deepest
cistern
filled with water.
I am keeping quiet.
But one day
the forest will talk about me.

*

Huutokoski

Here in the forest's
dry-muzzled summer
my thoughts were aroused to defiance,
the heat threw into my senses
a shadow all too dark.

*

You smile at
my little matchstick poems.
Their harmlessness has become legendary.
But it is better to have a box of them in one's pocket
than to sleep with ten fire extinguishers in the house.
They have made do
with brightly illuminating my face when they are lit
– and then going out.

*

God.
We wander in your light
in order to grasp your impossibility.
It swings
like an arc lamp in the storm
sending giant shadows dancing
over our motionless houses.

*

1.

I am an over-civilised
mouse.
Take me in the flat of your hand,
feel how I twitch and tremble
with nerve-reactions.
Life
thousand-fingered
strums
its cats' waltz
in my ear.

2.

I have only *one* thought.
If life picks up its scent
it will crush me.
My soul is nothing but trust.
If it lets me down
I will have spasms of hunger in a flourbin,
will leap unprotected by instinct
straight into the fire.

*

I am greedier for my welfare
than the ant is for the grass-blade.
If anyone's hand comes too near me
I spew ant-piss.
My whole being cranes up on two legs with quivering antennae.
My abdomen bends forward in a bow.
Under the lens you can see my spite in all its glory.

*

The Goods Wagon

I have been shunted onto the wrong track
and stand, a lonely wagon at the buffers.
Grey, I look in at the yellow edges of the forest.
I stand in the rain – the twilight dilates
but I will never reach my destination.

*

What I wrote
was a romantic compulsion.
I wanted to be imprisoned in
the dying shimmer
of a word,
to raise the echo of a past emotion.
I wanted to escape
to the world of the forest,
its dark meditations,
to find
satiety in a beast-like dream.

But luckily imagination's silver ring
fell from my finger.
The horizon of flying images
has grown dark.
In the mirror of a magic lake
the light grows fainter and will not return.
Only thought lingers,
doubly dear to a freed eye.

*

Melody

A bird's warble flies
like a swivel-bait cast over waves.
A splash of the morning light's gold leaf
around giddying rotation
spun out
into the very fibre of disappearance.

*

In Rome

In Rome the heat strikes rings in lime-dry air
the eye is blinded
and the soul's dust cakes one's eyebrows.

In the shadow of the arch I stand as on a mountain's shoulder
facing the sea of sun, and the fountain's splashing reaches me
with noise and voices from the dark, much-changing faces of life.

All the gaudy baroque droops like chrysanthemums in the heat.
Imperceptibly time boils dry
like the moisture in the marble basin – sucked up and forever
          renewed.

There behind drapery the coolness of a church's nave
and the body's yearning slinks in like a lizard over chiselled
          stone.

                    *

As distant as the sun is from the winter blaze in a red cloud,
as distant as – ! Day has altered to evening and the rosy shimmer
becomes magic darkness. Silently memory still tours
along roads whose dust
constantly recalls things that are lost.

Memory's veil, at first transparent as the wave of heat above
          clear fire,
grows heavy and opaque as the shadow in a ravine.
The sheer ravine of time
plunges straight into our souls.

Beaten in the iron of terror they intercept a sound
that echoes in our hearts' pulse; where and when?
The horn of Roland calls
deep within the light-branched, leafy forest.

                    *

Bust of Juno

Eye cooled by day, hair bound by marble
Junonian sun and the forehead's vault:
a mask for the depth of Hades' oblivion,
an underworld with river-waves
frozen in onyx and life's cyphers
dispelled like a dream –
Nothing will paralyse the power of the dumbness
unjoined by commanding times far hence upon the marble.
Nothing will kindle the fire
in her eyes; with her soul turned away,
swathed in the mantle of time's distance
she meets, powerful in resemblance, day's sun.

                         *

Longing appeals at heart to the change in all things.
The deed, once lofty and sun-illumined
is turned to a vessel consecrated in the darkness of the obscure
          past.
And the life which still like Pallas stands forth from the god's
          helmet
will soon radiate from a world, metamorphosed by visions,
          embraced by death.
Time, forever ready to create
in our place the greatness that evades us,
makes us all, on the front we occupy,
into stubbornly silent deserters, happy in longing.

                         *

The eyelids stiffen. Liver-brown shadows gather
under the eye.
The heart
pumps the aching blood of fear. A void
expands infinitely –

In the brain, a windless murmuring.
The eye looks in a mirror
as sick and smarting as a salt steppe.
A movement! And chaos
floods through your veins, shrouding
your body in a veil of blind pain.

*

The poverty that came to me
in silent years of childhood
is the treasure I covetously hoard.

The wheel-ruts of the slow roads,
the drying-hurdles steaming in the evening sun,
the mist over the lake
conceal what I hardly know how to miss:
conceal my sense of loss itself.

O rich inheritance of poverty.
Out of loyalty's unequivocal heart
the star has risen.
Its name is constancy.

*

Towards Ithaca

In sleep he is borne by waves
homewards where night and north
sweep space and immovably
    the constellation of Heracles
    raises its lever.

Is borne away by complete oblivion,
rich, powerful, weaving patterns of sound
squandering the nets of time
   swell sinking
   beneath its own fate.

He is borne so he shall not be
where flames lick up from Eos' dawn;
only homewards and nightwards –
   the sleep of gods
   'most akin to death'.

Chante-clair

High in November day flames your golden trumpet.
O herald, many times before now
your sentinel's cry has summoned men
to strife – and proudly kindled
the fire in their minds and their impatient fighting spirit:
Still in your cry
the banner of revolt flutters before the rebel,
the clear voice of lofty obedience
is announced
to willing hearts.
– Borne far away across the dying coxcombs of the echo
on the dizzying hunt for fortune
you are
the first message to strike home;
at the door of pale suffering and treachery,
the last warning –

The Heart

The longer life continues
the more like a dream
it becomes.
Heart, sore pressed,
soon you will rest unburdened beneath
oblivion's heaviest garlands
with the sparing blossom of memory.
All will exist only as the guest
and closest friend of death.
Yet – undying ivy will guard
the room of your pain.

*

Poets
compelled to poetry!
The blind satisfaction,
recognition sweet as the scent
of lily-of-the-valley, gentle but numbing,
said nothing to you.
You, that lived
on sparing, inaccessible insight:
bitter roots
of a soil dragged
from afar as though in defiance
of the nearness of that sea
stingily tended to earthly needs –
You, fishermen by a storm-heavy coast,
faces flushed with cold,
day-labourers of uncertainty,
patient tillers of poetry's Aran!
Your table unacquainted with victuals
that are not the product of your spirit's power.
You, poets
of the difficult school!

Oedipus at the Sea

Here on the shore of the shadowless
the shadow fly –
You touch me with unfamiliar hands,
feel my face as though you yourself were blind
and with a blind man's groping fingers sought
someone. At your touch I am
like a child –
around unkempt, grey-grown beard
you flutter mercifully,
tug at it in play.
Why can I not see you? Yet see you,
see you, sensing your depth.
Gentle as the repetition in a nurse's songs
with their more direct way
to the heart –

The misery of a human life
weighs lightly, O sea, in your embrace.
The two Nereids *All Things Must Pass* and *Sleep While There Is
        Time*
strew your bed with windwashed asters and fragrant mint.
The mist kisses one of your eyes,
the sun the other.
The night manifests its reconciliation in golden text.
However nimbly the Fate spins her thread in the here and now
for you she will always be too late,
and her action in vain.
Here on your shore
with my feet finally tamed,
here I sense that the bitterness in my life
is not towards you, that it is not you
that sickens my spirit. All that flees
to you finds a refuge.
You: who bid complaint be silent
with your hand gently laid upon the lips of lamentation,
with a divinity in your depths –
I see in everything not what it is
but what it means.
I wish that I lived in some context.

I wish that words
would find their way to me: vermin huddled beneath a stone.
There is life beneath a stone and the form of the most high
dwells in all that there is room for in this world.
That which is inside is easy.
It is as easy as Ariel and the west wind:
goes sweeping through every kernel, every word.
From the underworld nothing can be saved.
But spring is a launching board for all that goes outwards.
There death's trademark is valid as any other.

O Bridge of Interjections...

O bridge
of interjections,
you that pass over half of life in silence
and half of death
and yet are filled with life and death,
you that like a river reflect the banks
announcing their depth
without revealing or betraying
what is hidden by merciful trees
at the water's edge,
I will go your way like a Moslem
who approaches the mosque with covered head
led astray neither by what lies to the right or the left of him.

I will adorn my ear with sounds
that are audible only at sunrise
or towards nightfall, when each star sets out its bowl
to catch a sprinkling of the inaudible.
And I will adorn my eye with light
disclosing things that can be neither hidden nor seen,
such as breathe their scent from a distance
and cannot be lifted up and placed here or there,
since they remain with me always
wherever I am –

Among those lofty things
there is neither you nor I nor anyone else,
neither love, passion, jealousy nor revenge.
There is absolutely nothing to lay us bare
or give us occasion for arrogance or humiliation.
Those lofty things soar towards us
on the wings of interjections, transparent as the dragonfly's:
she glows with all that is behind her or ahead of her;
colourless in herself, each moment paints her anew.
They are like a tranquil air in which scents thrive.
One breathes them in as on a forest path.
But the sea, too, the rock and the storm are lifted
on the wings of interjections.

Whoever is versed in them
is like a skilful spinner: from matted wool comes flowing yarn.
O, is it really necessary to heap up facts?
Then I am lost. In facts I was imprisoned.
What speaks through me now is merely what
is present in any moment,
like rainwater in a crevice: it has gathered there
and dries up again in order to return.

Long we go bowed under the weight of circumstances.
One senses them everywhere – like the members of a jury
they judge us, acquitting or convicting us.
As long as we live we stand like prisoners at the bar.
O who can plead in his own defence other than
in a thoroughly inadequate fashion?
On whose side is the law, on whose true love?
These are questions that cannot be settled at once,
but must constantly be reiterated in the world of the half-
       hearted.
The defier and the conciliator
dwell in the same breast, in the same heart's chamber,
forever pursuing the same exchange of opinions.
In the long run we all lose out.
For what we win we allow to slip through our fingers
and what we lose comes back to us again.
In the degree to which we give it up for lost, it returns.
It returns by way of the loss that makes us reconciled.
It returns by way of the loss that makes us dream purer dreams.

It returns by way of the loss that makes us think truer thoughts
            and will better actions.
Verily: no one can say 'I have won!'
For no one wins in the end, but everyone loses,
loses until they are conscious of it and realise
that only by way of loss can the flood of things that are lost
be stemmed. It is so simple. Tears are the nervous spasm
of our desire to hold onto something, they are the child who
            refuses to see
that the sense of loss gives to life its deepest substance.

One can find nothing in life
unless one finds those words
that are transparent with
what the spirit has in common with everything and everyone.
One can find nothing unless one is able to weave oneself
a net that fits every sea and every river.

In interjections I have found a strong thread
that has been dipped in the pitch of eternity – in interjections,
            which are born
like the spider's web in the light of morning:
constantly at breaking-point, it often tries the eye of the
            beholder,
but it holds the spider, its creator,
as the world holds God. What does it matter
that much of it is torn to shreds? It matters nothing!
As long as the thread holds its creator.
I found the pitch-thread of eternity in the spider's web and in
            those interjections
which, dipped in my heart, held fast
even when its blood flowed hottest.

When the lover makes those long pauses between the words of
            love
those pauses that rest in the present like a butterfly on a hot
            stone,
without desire, need or purpose,
he is outside desire
and is in acceptance, in which his soul rests, open.
As after a violent downpour the sun shines more intensely
than it does on a cloudless day, so our lives are most intense

the moment we set ourselves free and stop thinking about
        purposes.
There is always something melancholy about one who is setting
        out on an expedition.

Why does the soul in his eyes seem to renounce
the result in advance? why does the moment of decision
make his stomach turn?
Where does this weakness come from? It creeps out of his soul,
        whispering: 'renounce'.
Renounce! You must admit that – if, like a parachutist, you took
        the risk –
only then did you really feel free.

There is within all of us something
that is too fragile not to break,
too fragile or too inexpedient.
Are we therefore to condemn it?
Complete expediency would never
find its way to the life that is more than cause and effect.
Complete expediency is not possessed
by the ox under the yoke, not even by the machine.
The ox contains that which is animal and is not the beast of
        burden.
The machine contains the incomplete, which is the human being.
Expediency can make no decisive contribution
to the argument about what our lives are worth.
No: sickness, want and hope –
that is life and its redoubts, never surrendered.

Let us therefore not condemn that which has made us
        vulnerable,
made us fall out with life and brought us face to face with the
        thieving brats of reality.
The wound proves that there was something
which went beyond the bounds of necessity, something
which demanded more and found less,
was a squandering of energy until reality
converted it into blind weakness.
To me the quarry is free when it is hunted
in mortal terror by a goading pack.

To me the murderer is free when, his soul on tenterhooks,
he awaits the ring at the doorbell,
the quite ordinary ring of an errand boy at the door with a
      delivery
from the grocer's shop around the corner –
and then another ring, one quite out of the ordinary, one that
      mercilessly
shoots the bolts of existence, discloses
the next step as a 'come with us' – the soft purring
of the police car from the street sounds like something in a
      dream –
This is a freedom you cannot escape!
A freedom which leads to something greater, something
      inconceivable.
One that will perhaps finally release
the most intense delight a human being can attain: the smile that
      nothing will be able to avert –

In the twilight of the gaol
on the stone floor, pressed
against damp walls and with the cell bars
like a cool and indifferent thought, irrelevant,
I felt for my companion in misfortune the kinship
common shame bestows.
For in a cell there is no concealing
the obvious. In gaol
a man goes free of condemnation and only
the unease of his own conscience examines
what is concealed
behind the ever more tightly knit
meshes of the interrogation. Fear and unease
about the inadequate weapons of cunning and watchfulness
construct a shared world
of hours that melt like hot tin.
Yet, when the fear grows less, even gaol
has its view of eternity
and over its walls, dark with twilight, falls
the shadow of the peace that is granted
to those who rest beneath the open sky.

Never will I forget
how well we got along

over our games of chess: the squares
scratched out on the stone floor with a pin,
the pieces made with cardboard torn
from an empty cigarette carton. Bent
over those scratched squares we found
a peaceful crevice in the now,
a field for the tournament of thought
and at times we would forget
that the morrow had already been lost
before our surroundings let go
their grip on us.
The knowledgeable thief entertained us
with songs from far and near,
always came back
from interrogation having confessed new crimes,
always calculating
what they would cost him in months
of life; yes, truly
justice did not scorn
the widow's mite –
Never will I forget
how dear hands sent me
the book about Watteau with its pairs of
silk-robed lovers in parks suffused
with the purple radiance from distant
sunsets.

Thus is our life – Vain
to try to set it on a course
for the better. There is
no "better" anywhere.
Fear and distress interrupted by
the occasional relief of
sleep and oblivion put man
in his rightful place. Whoever understands this
no longer negotiates with fortune
and the rainbow.

There is something that has gone –
A cloud has gone, a light, a cloud and a star.
I stand staring at that patch of emptiness
where once it was: a cloud has gone.

I do not know why this empty patch in the sky
should bring forth such emptiness within me.
I do not know why: since the cloud disappeared
I have felt a thirst that cannot be quenched.

My lips are dry, my soul rocks to and fro
like one whose abdomen hurts.
I know full well that everything is an illusion
and that life builds cycles of illusion.
And that all transformations simply illustrate
that here have we no continuing city.
In spite of every transformation we are kept
on a diet that is far too restricted: it satisfies us before we have
stilled our hunger.
Who but a conjuror could love reality for more than ten years at
a stretch?
What comes after that is nothing but repetitions, which give us a
certain degree of immunity,
but by no means indemnify us; on the contrary, although the
symptoms grow less noticeable, the disease penetrates
deep down.
Work, leisure, all that is measurable in purely external terms
becomes more significant and the emotions are now the great
stumbling-block we must overcome.
But we overcome them not at all, we merely conceal them,
conceal them from the sight of others and ourselves.
Increasingly we make life into a plan of action, a sphere of
activity.
The most precious and sensitive instruments have been lost in
the storm,
But we attempt to manage without them, we trust to our own
eyes.

Can we hold the course? Do we care whether we hold it any
more?
Chance and our eyes grow more and more closely wedded to
each other.
In this magnetic field everything is simpler.
Even the oarsman, aimlessly rowing, has a regard to the wind
and the waves.

Those who consciously describe themselves as corks before the
          wind do not become more so
than those who are, but are unaware of it...

To be poor is to be on the lookout –
We all stand in the queue ordained by necessity.
We do not know what it is we are queuing for, we join the queue
without knowing what the goods are worth:
desirable or not, it is all the same.
The queue forms like an ice-pattern on a window
and is longest
when one is looking forward to what one cannot get.
Patiently the days of our lives unfold,
frozen and wretched,
soon hopeless – and yet we go on with them
just for the enjoyment of waiting – and when we ourselves are no
          longer waiting
for the enjoyment of waiting with those who still are.
We warm ourselves at the glow of hopefulness as greedily
as the street-vendor at his brazier.

Toughness our most efficient stimulant,
a decoction of 'perhaps', 'you never know',
'as well here as there', 'it could well be'.
Joined together by words and thoughts like a wire
the queue winds
binding our hearts somewhere
between belief and scepticism,
'good luck' and 'that's the end of that'.

Thus we are incapable of dying
and what we live by is what we are unable to cope with.
It is so simple – in this greyness
dwell harmonies, sweet scents that make
our spirits tremble, our hearts hammer
obstinately – in painful contradiction
to all that we know –

To be poor is to be on the lookout,
on the lookout for life and death, to sense
how closely they follow each other

into our hearts, as closely as the windshadows on a flag.
Only the hunter knows the way the quarry moves,
the detours it will make, where he will find it,
only the hunter knows, and the hunter is life.
Our hearts are marshes on which shots ring out,
but we see nothing of the quarry that is felled.
That is the hunter's secret and a secret too
is the deep silence that is death's echo –

Like a roe-deer oneness had fled from me –
And where I walk the paths are muddled together
and all the trees look the same.
But however far I may have gone astray in the exitless,
to you, wanderer, it will one day be disclosed,
to you, that wander under happier skies
where confusion's film of blood does not obscure your sight,
that here once the foot of a roe-deer left its imprint,
here in the valley of oneness and longing.

O bright valley, resting always further away
than thought and eye are so quick to believe!
O bright valley, there you are, glimmering in daylight more
        clearly
each time the mists of vanity are dispelled.
The wearier grow one's steps the more clearly sounds
the purling of springs, the light across your meadows
and the water of the unattained rock cools
the throats of those who succumb but never
lose sight of their vision –

Long I sat on the bench of life
looking as though I were not looking,
saw the columns, supply vans,
heard the rumble of tanks, the frenetic din of engines.
The man at the wheel: stone gods, totem poles,
isolated, exalted in their din, while the caterpillar tracks
scraped out listlessly burrowing claws in the dust.
How long I sat there looking
looking as though I were not looking
looking as one looks at the crowd on a platform
keeping one's eyes peeled for the one whom one is to meet, only
        for the one whom one is to meet,
seeking a voice in the tumult –

Among leaves that have lost their sheen,
among flowers that have lost their colour –
Within the perianth they have their glow
and decay has its incense
of the past – a gentleness without limits –
So listen inwards, to what does not believe,
does not hope and does not remember; a web
of dead things that have lost their forms
and are merely air or nothing!
They have drowsed away from them, they have slept,
slept long, alas, even during their lives they were sleeping
a sleep full of dreams about something
that never was –
Someone is loitering outside,
creeping in at your doors –
in search of warmth and company,
bread for his hunger –
Why does he not just come right in and say what it is he wants?
Why is he creeping about outside?
Drive him away: he has dark designs.
Chase him away! But he is not there. Where is he? Where has he
              vanished to?
But I know there is someone creeping about outside,
someone to whom I can give neither bread nor warmth –
Is it hope, dark hope?

Strew ashes, abundance of ashes,
ashes on the hard-frozen field,
on the winter snow, so that it melts away
laying bare the brown earth!
For you have an errand to me as you have to others,
sun!
All your mail has the word
Urgent marked on it.
Urgent – such a hopeful word,
so warm, when sent in your letters:
your beams!

How often the gold text in your stamp is borrowed
for things and communications of such little urgency!
Your message passes through so many
bitter intermediary hands that

– when finally it reaches us –
we are unable to decipher the garbled text.
But sometimes it amuses you
to throw your letters down to us
directly from above
and then there is a scent as delicate
as marsh violets –

Spring comes so quietly:
all the herb-gardens already hold
their seeds – all the herb-gardens
the gardener loves before all else.
Filled with the tension of expectancy
the rustle of the seedsticks
in the bag – now they have come to rest
in the soft folds of the soil, sealed in there.
He loves them best:
the sharp and the soft,
the light and the dark.
He loves them for the sake of their bitterness
and for their sweetness –
abundance here is paired
with fine discernment
and an aroma as full as that of the rose
here has its nearness to victuals, the frugal necessities of life.

Interjections,
forgotten by sound
possessed by light!
You are the girl where she sits
in the arbour's shade, bowed over the book that is making her
          heart flutter.
Now she averts her gaze, her eyes pause for a moment
seeking coolness on roses and blue lupins
to avoid those pages that come flooding over her
with too great a confusion.
When the voice of her mother calls her to the table that is ready
          laid
her own voice answers in faltering tones –
She has been far away. Will she finally have the strength
to get up and push away
the soft branches – ?

Or: you are the youth, when during heart-tearing exertion
he shapes words on his lips, words he makes as humdrum as
          possible
in order to hide his insecurity, his fear, despair –

O interjections
you possess the shortest way to renewal –
you know corruption.
Light as butterflies
you steer from flower to flower.
So much trouble with the manifold
in order to attain the unique!
There is no shorter way
than you:
like the arrow quivering in the target you have already reached
          your goal
in the honey sac –
the cup of bitterness
O interjections, there you float:
keywords of chance, rinsed clean by the storm,
transparent from the wind,
butterfly-wings capsized on a stone cairn
merely commemorating what remains of
the flight of countless butterflies in the sun –

SOLVEIG VON SCHOULTZ

30. XI. 1939

That day, too, became night.
The light our lantern threw
Past house after empty house
Shook on asphalt, empty and blue.

We walked on windows' torn corpses,
On a broken splintering seam
Carefully, as if somewhere
There lay hidden a scream.

But the street was already dead.
Walls from wounds grown grey
Stood with grief-dimmed eyes.
Here children stood yesterday.

Acrid and alien
The smoke from fires passed us there.
The window nearest our lantern
Gaped speechless and bare.

Curtains stiff with soot.
A night wind made them roam.
They lifted like black wings,
Birds without a home.

My Time Is Brief

The holy disquiet knocked at my door.

'I haven't the time, I'm baking my bread,
the dough is rising, the oven is red.
Wait, as you've had to wait before.'

The holy disquiet went from my door.

The holy disquiet tried my lock.

'Don't come near me, my child is fresh,
It's sucking my blood, my marrow, my flesh.
Leave me alone with my son, I say.'

The holy disquiet went away.

The holy disquiet stood in my house.

'The chimney is smoking, haven't you seen?
I'm sweeping my neighbour's kitchen clean.
My children are crying. But nice you should call.'

The holy disquiet turned from my hall.

The holy disquiet sat by my bed.

'Oh, is it you? I'm too tired now,' I said.
'I would have loved you young or dead.
Was there something you wanted? My time is brief.'

The holy disquiet left, trembling with grief.

The Water Butt

The water butt by the corner
has an eye that I love.
In the morning it laughs
when the aconites borrow its mirror
    adorning themselves for the butterflies,
in the heat it lies shadowy, out of reach,
    talking to the honeysuckle's leaves,
sometimes it plays with the children
    curling pygmy waves for their bark boats,
but only at night, when children and grown-ups are gone,
does the eye come wide awake
grow clear and listen,
open itself to the darkness above the pines,
in a cool lap girding
Aldebaran.

Accept It

Accept it, God.
I give you my defeat.
Take in your strong hands
the knife that cut.
Cut deeper,
cut bolder. I am said to be hard.
Prise my shell loose,
the dark shell I carry.
Force in your knife
and tell me, God: is the kernel there?
I close my eyes, await the knife.
Cut.

Prayer

Linger, bread, between my hands,
Give warmth of life, O you, divinely generous,
and let me put my cheek against your rough bark,
faithful bread.

How happy your brown scents are:
corn grown sweet in sun, dark kiln, the rattle of grain.
Blood has flowed into you from the earth's entrails,
blushing bread.

Pagan women shaped you with their spells
and Christian crosses set a ring around your holy bed:
dark weapons were surrendered before your eye,
mortals' bread.

Venerable bread, you that saw the origin of the ancient families,
you, born from soil, interred in soil and born again,
do not forsake us on the last day,
merciful bread.

She-Bird

Like a woman, hesitant and caught
amidst life's blond and downy-feathered years,
a mother, bowed at low beds, who forgot
to look up where the midday sun appears,
she upped and left her warm and twilit nest,
now grown too small for all her brood and her.
She found a truth where she'd refused to trust.
She found that summer had stepped far, O far.

Her feathers were still sleek and brilliant,
her breast still soft from nights of harmony.
And suddenly she knew just what life meant:
one brief, hot summer, woman, you have left.
One brief, hot summer. Hurry. You are late.
And then? The journey that is mystery.
A day in early autumn – clear, mercy-bereft.

The Woman of Samaria

At the sixth hour our thirst enlarged
and the man in my bed bit my heel
and said: water.

And I sounded hollow as my pitcher
and my throat was sticky as from sacrificial blood
and my loathing was like sweat.

And I bore my pitcher to Jacob's well
throughout years of clear, red hopelessness:
to thirst in the midst of thirst.

And lo, a stranger sat on the well's stone rim
beneath the merciless dark blue
wrapped in the folds of his rest.

And the man's voice sank into my pitcher's clay:
if you drink this water
you will thirst to eternity.

That was at the sixth hour. The sun was absorbed
into his eye and grew as narrow as a spear
urgently burning its path.

And the man stepped into my gaze
and men stood concealed there, he touched them
and walked past their ashes.

That was at the sixth hour. And my thirst
lay exposed as a riverbed, dark brown
in its arid immensity.

By the panting furrow he bent down:
I will give you the springing water
I will give you living water.

And the coolness sank from my throat to my heel.
I hear the aching tremor from deep within me.
My brim is dark with moisture.

I will rise and go. I do not know where.
A sea has been born in me. I do not know how.
One thing I know: living water.

The Heart

We gave her seed; not much,
but enough so she would not grow tired;
water we gave her, a thimbleful,
to remind her of the source.
We opened the door a tiny way,
so the heavens would smite her in the eye
and we fastened a bit of mirror to her cage
so she could look straight into the cloud.
Quiet she sat, with flickering wings.

That way she sang.

Nocturnal Meadow

Here, this meadow:
the small, bright clearing of awareness
fenced and fertilised, mown to the furthest corners
where the dog's muzzle of night-scented herbs nosed round his
     knees
round the boot-strides of safety.

Intrusive rustlings around scant clearing
covetously bent black walls inwards
invisibly crawled and gorged
and eyes watched, claws sharpened, wings rose
hear the warning rattle, the raucous gutturals of fate.

But still his meadow:
the light bottom of the deep-murmuring well.
And like a glass-clear cube eternity shot
straight up with spiracles at the Plough
as it moved on its mighty wheels.

Woman Cleaning Fish

With my long brown arms
I hurl entrails into the sea
wind and perch-scales fight around my throat
seaweed washes my toes
the corpses yawn
– there! My heart quivering with white lumps of fat
has taken a nose-dive; a scream
– you, omnivorous stomach grinding down like and unlike
sway in the seaweed
I don't want to see you
– you, yellow gall, you insult to the sun
stinking bitterness
may the old corpse-crayfish take you
take the snaking subterfuge of my intestines
the cowardly constipation of mouldy memories
– with my long arms

I hurl the seagulls' brazen laughter
tear slimy membranes
snort my blood, I will scrunch and rinse
vomit out into contemptuous cold and salt-green:
neat white flesh and a few angry spines.

The Sewing Machine

Here, in a secret alcove between the laundry basket and the
        kitchen
the objects that were hers crowded together under a brown
        wooden cover:
the trusty, sharp scissors that cut dreams to ribbons,
the infinite patience of the spools
and the small pins with the motley-coloured heads of countless
        worries.
Here her years ran along sprouting seams
smoothed beneath a dutiful thimble.

What held them together was this: patched-up sheets,
that the worn can old be made to do, that the hopeless can be
        rescued.
But slowly rescue became more difficult and meaningless:
the aching of the wheel, that had been there all along,
pressed up through this: this is how it is supposed to be,
and grew dark and turned to suspicious bewilderment
and she stopped her treading and saw she was alone.

Patience

Behind what you say there is something else.
The visible is crazed by alleyways.
Scent of prophylactic herbs,
grape hyacinths' courage.
Behind your fragments all is whole.
Hidden horses on nocturnal meadows.
Smiles, alerted, at our ignorance.
Death is only a river flowing inward
towards the plain whose name is trust.

Loneliness and hunger are only now.
How will we recognise ourselves
in the hour our purpose is made known,
and there is nothing in vain?

Lazarus

Three days he had lain wrapped in his resolve
with dark stains in the region of his cere-cloth:
the eyelids: they had renounced everything,
lowered over stifled vanity;
the nose; its haughty monument
to evaporated memories of happiness
before the bitter lips dried up the tongue
repenting of its fluttering to and fro;
the ears: a final lock
behind which he was at last himself
in a cavern of astonished silence,
yet most silent of all his hands
with brooding knuckles: all is in vain.

Like a bulb beneath layers of the past
a memory wintered in his heart,
a small, whitish sliver of fear,
but even this was making ready to die.
When, through the caverns of silence, a blow reached him,
a trumpet of light, and he answered with silence
stiffening inside his averted shell

until the trembling lashed him again
the close pounding of alien light
and the sliver of fear swelled in his heart
and with his dead body Lazarus cried: *No.*

The trumpet of the command.
                    An unbearable pain
streamed in his limbs, a violent light
a death to light, the bursting of the stiff bandages –

                    Lazarus. Arise.

Tree

There is no other way than to become more tree.
Make it up with the soil. The soil: eternally the same.
The stones the same.
The gravel the same.
Nailed for all time to this: immovability.
To move in the tree's direction:
deeper down.

Can a tree that loves storms become a storm?
The tree can do no other than to rend its crown.
Be shaken through by cries
the tree the nailed-fast soughing
born to be tree
drives its longing inward
into the form of tree.

The dark-shadowed grows broader. Broad
the pillar descends and without vertigo sings greater
towards the cloud its heart of leaves
rest for all that travels
safety for birds and for the seeds
forever in motion
deep in its innermost wood.

There is no way than to become more tree.

The Pike

I?

I am the pike.
Yellow-ringed green and black:
tough-tailed triumph.
To me unlimited power is given.

Who are you?

I took your bait.
Its seduction gleams inside me.
Never think I have regrets.
I wanted. I took.

True: it hurts
under my powerful heart.
But rarely: in soft spasms.
What do you want of me? Sport?

Do not think you have me.
It amuses me to come when you call.
Sometimes, to strike terror into your heart
with my sudden-stealing back.

But away!
Away from your evil eye
in tail-tenebrous whistle and whirl
nosediving into night
– my spawning-time's shadowclear hunting-ground
my quivering small-fry my ripping jaws
my arrow-flight's hissing will –
Go on.
Tear your barb under my wild heart.
Is it death I have swallowed?

But will you take me alive?
Never.

The Cloud

Slowly the cloud came loose and drifted over the river,
the baleful cloud the landscape had dreamt.
It moved in melancholy towards another night.
In the dream the riverbanks had flowed out into the water.
They stopped, still afraid, in their flight.
Colourless light flowed in over low reeds,
sparkling in the meadow's rough stubble.

A buzzard burst from the banks' uncertainty and rose
higher, until he had conquered the meadow
higher, until he alone possessed the morning's cries
and higher, until he lay down on his strength and floated
with the brazen sun concealed in his wings:
grey and brown quiverings of light.

June Sauna

This is the body's joy this side of age and sex:
to curl one's toes against a sooty wall
to stripe the skin of one's back against a baking bench
to roll shadows around in the pit of one's stomach

to be stabbed in the eye by the peephole, small, rage-boiling
         green
the frayed dotted curtain
the inquisitive clump of nettles
to snort at a hissing alder whisk

to gasp for blessed air by the steaming groan of the stones
distil guile from one's skin
scoop innocence from the water butt
to be smoothed childlike and shining wet

to crawl glowing away from the little sootblack island
absent-mindedly chew sorrel
ice-cold whortleberry flowers
whistle at the wood-dove's weeping music

and behind a bush perform one's evening prayer.

The Pasture

The lantern is small
for those who must walk through the pasture at night
bobbing it lights

by glimpses and hardly at all
bares itself
followed by unfathomable eyes

sends sudden beams quivering:
a coarse hoof gleams in the mire

a step away that which has no name
jostles in masticating darkness
moans, shifts dully,
crushing twigs beneath its weight

arches the whites of its eyes
the lantern lights by glimpses

when it has gone
the pasture will be dark as before
the millennia will continue to murmur
and the tangled spruce trees will rock to and fro
their view concerning the stars

Pain

You threw me off.
A hail of stones
lashed my face and your hooves
vanished in glowing embers.

I know you will return
quivering, lathered.
And I shall mount you:
my spurs thirst for your hide
I shall mount you: tame your rebellion between my knees
and we shall travel forward together
as one
tautly, silently stepping,
one for one.

The Room Overlooking the River

The only calm is to break one's calm,
to know when the water grows stagnant and acquires a smell of
        death.
False is the calm on a windless shore
and the house of safety has closed-up shutters.

But give me this room of river-blue air
with walls that are still empty,
this naked floor of boards
running together towards one thing: the window,
open to the flowing water of night and day.
There deceit will be washed away
in small, wicked eddies
and day and night will sough away
small pieces of myself.
Until I am as naked and hard as the floor overlooking the river
until chance takes wing like clouds of autumn finches
until I stand open like a window
on the brown sun of change.

Three Sisters

The woman stooped down and picked up her child
and her hair fell over her face
and inside her a little old woman
withered and clear-eyed
stooped down with trembling head
to pick up her knitting
and inside her
a young girl stooped down to pick up her doll
with tender hands

three sisters
who would never see one another.

Old Woman

The head had a life of its own:
on a withered neck
it raised its tower of experience.
The roof of grey grown thin
crowned its weatherbeatenness
watery recesses
stared from networks of care
small elephant-grey stones
hard with wisdom.
The head had an age of its own.
The head: a tyrant.

The body: a subjugated land
the shoulders modestly young
with dry, white skin.
The body, delayed in dreams
of waterlilies and blood.

An Unknown Beak

An unknown beak pierced my breast
and there it stayed while the bird drank
and there I stayed
almost without pain
for as long as the bird sucked my blood with its beak
sucked deeper
I did not know
if I had bled to death or become a bird.

Rest

Inside unhappiness it is quiet, everyone has gone past,
all doors are shut, you hear no sound.
Sparse furnishings, unaired darkness
but rest,
face and body against hard floor
but rest
and a strange dream about God.

Sisyphus

Thus far was he shown mercy
or its opposite:
at the moment he had heaved the boulder to the top
relief raised him up
straightened his back
forgetfulness filled his head
with a thin cool breeze
and this moment lasted just long enough
for him to regain faith and apply his weight
to the boulder again.

The Cell

Gradually he learned it.
He was very seldom there.
Sometimes, when his head hit the wall
he would return to his body
and rediscover terror.
Someone had permitted his escape.
Perhaps it was God.
He travelled far and wide.

Conversation

For forty years they had lived with each other
and the language was growing harder and harder to understand
at first they had known a few words
later on they made do with nods:
bed and food.
For forty years they had coped with the day-to-day.
Their faces grew calmer, like stones.
But sometimes a chance interpreter appeared:
a cat, an unusual sunset
they would listen with an air of unease
try to answer
                    they were already speechless.

Then

And then, when God had burned down on every branch
man stood
a Christmas tree bereft of needles
looking around in the daylight
dimly remembering
something that had made him shine.

The Dolls

But when she looked at all those years
she found they had turned into dolls, with rigid eyes
some dozing, some wide and transparently awake
some dressed in finery, with undulating hair
some naked, with breasts and slender arms
but all unable to move, all in a row
    she stuffed them into a sack and pulled the cord
    now they are gone
                now they are truly gone

The Poor Man's Lamb

The poor man's only lamb slept in the poor man's lap
and was like a daughter to him
eating out of the poor man's bowl near the poor man's beard
warming her wool at the poor man's sorrowful heart
roughly licking the constant hand that firmly
held on to his sole possession:
his daughter.

  Hold her trotters firmly, the lamb is dancing in a dream
  where? On the rich man's farm where the lambs are many
  the gambollings quivering-high and the air untrammelled
  where the lambs drink muzzle to muzzle from the spring
  and lie down with blissful trotters
  on green meadows where they find rest.

Death is like King David
with his melancholy crown of gold
death gathers treasures and gives nothing away
but even death will have to answer
for what it has done to the poor man.
Only the lamb has rest
the lamb has escaped from her father
and the pen of her loyalty.

The Angel

On my shelf stands a little angel of wood
with gilded wings and a halo like a hat.
I was given him once a long time ago
by someone who believed in angels
  right then I needed
a guardian angel (it's a need that has grown no less).
He has had a hard job.
  He has lost
one of his wings, he has fallen off the shelf
during the struggle with Satan (not a stranger here)

and his gold paint has flaked off.
 But his obstinacy
is as great as Satan's, he goes on standing
where he promised to stand, a little angel
with a broken wing and a halo like a hat.

The Burning Glass

As when in spring
one focuses the sunlight in a burning glass
watching the heat grow narrow
the paper blacken
and a little dot inside
begin to glow
so also should despair
burn holes in silence.

The Pole Star

The pole star in the universe clings to itself
however much the earth may turn
however the stars may be confused
the pole star stands by its constancy.
So do I.
If I steer a steady course
nailed to the one thing I know
the uttermost and only thing I know
 I can exchange glances with God.

Easter Suite

I

In childhood's days Good Friday fastened still
as did the sky above the hill's strong pines
deep blue and brightly scrubbed and without end.
One wore one's Sunday best, as did the sky,
and was constrained to silence, and no games.
Brown fronds of willow stood in glass-blown jars
whose water contained ice, first buds of spring
that waited to be free to shed their scales.
Beneath the stones on hillsides lizards lay
in frozen boulders waiting for the sun.
We spoke low-voiced, and our own waiting grew
in shining expansivity, and made
our long Good Friday more prolonged. No games.
It was so still one walked about on tiptoe,
listening. But what happened then occurred
So deep and still that nothing could be heard.

II

How can one not submit?
No gaze is so radiant and dark blue
penetrating everywhere, into the snowdrift
that, hissing, collapses into the ice
that waits with red lakes, and into the heart
where winter still holds out
      how can one not submit?

III

What death lures us with: so easy to live
when one is dead. Simply to cease to hear
and cease to see. Simply to seal the chinks
around a dark, eternal mirror-calm.
O peace, O wondrous inward-moving peace
O lack of dread. To turn one's eyes within

on depths that do not move, and never will,
and merely silently reflect themselves.
O to walk among all living creatures
and be dead.

IV

This fearful leavetaking of winter
the pulse of revolt beating and beating
just as much inside us as outside us
already the willows are reddening
already the water is clattering under the snow
the light compels the transformation on us
unconcerned with what is dying
the ice is made to leave like love gone grey
there is no refuge
    death defends itself and makes the cold more keen.

V

The lower the sun
the bluer the ice, keener blue sword-sharp
the redder the catkins of the alder
the harder the birch-buds in the smoke from the sauna
Rigid, the buckthorn clutches towards the stone
but the snow burns like cold fire.

VI

No one heard the swans that night
but still the shore is white as outstretched necks
and the water on the melting ice dark metal
like the eyes of birds.

    Out of the sea of seals rises the Easter god
    with pike in his hands
    dark brown from solar laughter
    he breaks off a willow-fork
    he plods heavily in the snow
    he divines the water's path.

The willow-fork wrenches itself downwards
and stays impetuously turned
towards the secret things beneath the ground.

Where are the newborn lambs?
The ones that are newly broken forth
on high, trembling legs.
Let us see newborn lambs
now as the sun is deepened, hovering
low over the darkening ice on the lakes
now when the air is becoming a bubbling density
and the grouse are erupting over the floes.

BO CARPELAN

Lyric Suite

1

Like this unending line:
cheek, throat, road, horizon;
like a sleeper tensed between death
and life, with the tenderness of closed eyelids.
Like the joy in light footsteps,
like sun, wet leaves and air
and all old wellsprings' song of time,
beauty of summer, of pliant roads
and small, bitter herbs.
Like play of shadows on a hand at rest
and a day of heat, trees and swallows.
Like this unending line:
cheek, throat, road, horizon.

2

Now they die in a pendular longing,
the swift shadows. Farewells
fill the atmosphere with early ageing.
The invisible road is far too close
and the hand's repose has been annulled.
A song is growing in the vacuum of the sun
about the final shadow's silent passage.

3

Beyond the isolation of the fields, those dark shores
beyond the fields' glow, rocks and blasts of wind.
From deep wellsprings darkness burgeons forth,
chill as all that's utmost in the hour
and behind gatebars and a banging door
the frightened beat of hooves –
By dark waters, seared through with fire,
hear this storm coming out of the cathedral's cloak
this singing and abyss of silence.

4

Now every memory grows pale
the hand conceals no star –
Grief, berceuse and early dawning:
an atmosphere of loss
an atmosphere of shadows' empty play.

Like an Obscure Warmth

In the wool of the evening someone
with a lantern wanders by –

like an obscure warmth
lasting until dawn
is the pendulum's secret expectancy.

The Dreamer

The one who sows in the heavy soil of dreams
sees his face obliterated by the morning
remaining only as a memory in an impassive gaze

has no transition between life and life:
the closer to himself the more a stranger
slowly abandoned in the corridors of his veins.

From Variations

Like a stranger silence passes
through your skin, through a blue forest hall.
Further and further you wander without seeking:
a net of dreams, a stilled root
deep-hidden in timeless space, in timeless earth.

*

From your waiting no road grows.
The day melts like a voiceless bell –
hear it toll and you are among shadows,
ash drifting in the wind of time. Above you wheel
the plaintive birds of flight and silence
in endless rings above the onset of the dusk.

*

What is shadow? What your longing?
Rain of silence, autumn's beauty,
mist silver-grey above trees in flame,
no persecution, no death.

*

Confused, the pointsman spreads
his sleep over a snowless autumn,
over a hesitating, pliant spring.
All these down-grey days
are mixed with darkness or with longing,
along the gentle winters siding flames
the swiftly dying light of truth.
Handicraft for the night, plied by defeat!
Do you not surrender these innermost regions
when you wander in double form
between trees and people?

*

Near the fields, with her slightly faltering shadow
stooped over the ground, kneeling.
Alas, how many forsaken years
have carved their branches, drying rivers
in her averted skin?

And the forever returning birds,
the lingering voices, nights half-forgotten, what of this
is really strange to us? Her heavy heart
we bear beneath the bridge of our own blood
out towards the uttermost sea, the grip of
carelessly straying hands, resolver of the years'
dung and gifts.

*

The cry is prolonged into a face
obliquely borne through evening's lake.
What ought to be detected in the threat
of the swift twilight still burns
but is quickly, defencelessly over.

*

Alas, these town bells make a noise like children,
ancient, playing in the kerchief of the evening.
Black fields, people
move silent with secret sleighbells.
On his way through the saviour slows down
for a moment in his worn-out carriage.
Lakes slide into one another's shores.
Trees slide into one another's trunks.
Soon sleep and wakefulness will die away.
Voices that began their song between them
sink and rise like oarblades dipped and raised again
out across the surface of a silence mirroring nothing.

From Minus Seven

Birth

When I was born I returned to a world I thought I knew more
about than I did about my mother and father. Their earliest
conversations with me I found alien; as they stooped over me,
they submerged my gaze in shadow; I fell asleep, dreamed I
was a little infant. Was I metamorphosed in the dream? I woke
up crying?

F

A Night at the Opera

When the performance had only just started, my mother intervened for the benefit of my sister, who at that time was merely a walker-on in the crowd scenes. Armed with nothing more than high spirits she succeeded, after some difficulty, in getting up onto the stage, and during a break in the music, before the entrance of the hero, began to sing a little ditty, while my sister sobbed in the dusty wings, overcome with joy. In no time at all the audience had picked up the tune and were joining in my mother's singing with heart and soul. The entire house rocked to the sound of mighty music, and of all my family I was the only one to keep my head. At last I found the atmosphere too much, and made for the exit. As from the doorway I carefully observed the world below me, I saw the whole opera house swaying slowly to and fro like some drunken, luminous glass ball suspended from a thread formed of my sister's sobbing, the only sound that carried all the way to where I stood. I had some difficulty in keeping myself from crying.

The Fragrance of Snow

The fragrance of snow, like that of clean glass, is so imperceptible that only a written meditation on it can give any idea of its almost non-existent character.

Music and Words

As the conductor raised his baton I involuntarily rose to my feet in order to join in the beautiful main theme which came floating like a wide-brimmed hat out of the swaying, whispering orchestra on its thin mirror surface; but was unable to produce a sound. Not even when someone gave me a pen and a piece of paper, hastily produced, was I able to give satisfaction – there was no connection between this music and words. Had anyone really expected me to succeed? I shut my eyes, but my hand couldn't see to write. Gradually everyone left the concert hall, the lights went out and I was left alone, an old man, abandoned by music, abandoned by words.

The Dog

I once used to own a large dog – or was it blue? Every evening it used to take me out for walks, so I should get some fresh air. Its eyes reflected its sorrow at my growing older and larger. I, too, was affected by melancholy: I would rub my muzzle, dream about hunts far away, whimper in my sleep – my cheeks would sag down in heavy folds. One restless night my mother came in and found me lying in my basket, whining. She screamed, and I woke up. After that, we had no more dogs. Was it black, or was it blue? I miss its face, which once used to come so close to my own.

The Tortoise

Upon encountering me, he got down on all fours. When he was well clear of me again, he loped off, almost bounding. As I stood in my dark hallway, it occurred to me that he had done it out of loyalty. He had presumably taken me for a tortoise, and I had to admit that a cursory glance at my shell, my short legs and my wrinkled throat might well support such a thesis. But these things are merely the consequence of age. And there is certainly nothing the matter with my eyes.

Loneliness

Had it not been for the fact that I was so lonely, I would never have been able to endure this lack of human beings.

Horses

Horses, wildly vanishing in a cloud of dust.
Here on the verandah the heart still beats
with the flying echoes of hooves
red whirlpools through the dusk.

On Viewing Some Old Flemish Masters

1

The perspective is familiar. We wander through the room.
The landscape is transformed, only a part of life.
We sense it, unseen; and so it overshadows us.
Our blood complies with it, moving in total silence,
completing our outward vision in a world inwardly real.

2

She knows what sufferings she will meet.
Yet in her white, frilled collar she preserves her calm.
Her childlike hands too are at rest, and so they touch us
as we attempt to hide in details, remind us of
our childhoods, of the future, like the master, unknown.

3

The only and the only needed sign of love:
the nearness of the wife's hand to the husband's. In between,
the flower vase with its mirroring of an invisible window,
and the grey backdrop, life's tapestry: the backdrop
to our re-encounters which quietly they watch with their
         attentive eyes.

4

The evening grows still, of birds. Turned away
towards the interior of his room he registers our steps
as of those already dead, stumbling across his yard:
a tumult, alien to the sparing colours in his hand.

Elegy

Your hair is a constellation I lately saw transformed.
It lives, bleeding like a wounded beast
on the earth's field, in my innermost dream.
There it cuts the dark into stones and geometry.
No winds can reach you; you rest
beneath sand, silvered by sand. The darkness
falls, strikes me in my sleep; I turn
half on my side and embrace a death.
The wind from the sea lifts itself on its elbow,
pierces my breast through, echoes with slackened hands.
No river of blessing water
unites any more, in my heart, people and stars.
I see how once my soul, set free, on wings
sought its way towards a bounded, boundless sphere.
There, in the foam of the dark, your blood is spread like clotted
        spume,
is transformed, become a constellation round your death.
Asbestos-clad, rocket-like, your late-time sister attains her dead
        reflection.
Your hair is a constellation I lately saw transformed,
on a night when the heart tugs restlessly at its moorings
below the gaping jetties of the starry sky, below walls that break.

Ballad of the Lingerer

He wanders alone
by the sea's silence,
he wanders in his heart
while his blood moves
like the sea's waves;
his transformation begins
in the hours of darkness
touching his love
as the air touches water.
There on the sea
the silent vessels glide
that move his mind

towards distant regions.
First, the crossing!
Then memory, wingbreadth,
the carrying winds,
silence of forests.
He wanders alone,
a captive in space,
a part of his flight,
a stone of his way
yet still at home
in unknown regions
with this grief
that is the elements';
his birds scattered.
his cry silenced,
yet still a return
to all that is dreamed
and that lives in the earth,
that erects mountains,
that gathers the blood
like voices in towards death.
Soon his images will approach
like blind beggars
beside his hands,
beside the sea-coast's sands.

Shrink the World

On the hill, our hill
stands a tree
in the shadow, carved out of flying sunlight.
A larva sees the tree there as a form of darkness
and no clouds. On its scale of things
we get no further than dark and light.
Shrink the world!
I want to see the darkness on the hill, the darkness of the hill,
the darkness of all space and in that dark
the light of the ordinary, like a gleam
and the outline of your soul.

Silent Evening

No one comes near.
The room is bleeding
like a flower,
a mouth, silenced;

the sleeping infant
in the sleeping mother
turns
towards its image in the night;

snow is falling, effaced
by the wind
are the fumbling tracks
that lead out of my boyhood.

The words are trying to find their way
towards the centre of silence,
light as mountains
borne by the winds.

Farewell

Wider than the sea, deeper
than space

this farewell spoken when you return
and the grass's chill.

Autumn Walk

A man is walking through the woods
on a day of shifting light.
He encounters few people;
stops, looks up at the autumn sky.
He is making for the graveyard
and no one is following him.

The Mute Grass

The heart is not consistent with its bounds
nor the poem with reality
nor reality with God's dream.
What kind of dialogue is it that transforms one
without oneself being transformed?
Do not seek in the mute grass,
seek the mute grass.

From 73 Poems (1966)

1

Who was it said
that silence bears witness
to the unsaid?
Absent words
are absent.
So speak
in proportion to what
you cannot say.
Nothing
can be left unsaid
except through lack of skill
or through
wisdom.

9

Through the window
blitz-like
like a circular hole made by a weapon
a star;
through the hole the window's image,
a reflection,
in the window a circular hole.

41

The tree,
branched
light

43

Winter trees,
brittle, their stillness
I saw, did not see
when young.

47

I go
transforming myself
into the one who goes
beneath barely visible stars,
amidst dry leaves,
where we all,
in the end.

51

The wind
in the trees: silent rain.
I dream about father:
he is rowing out to fish
off a skerry far in the distance
never to
return.

58

The veins
beneath thin
skin,
the hand
on the quilt,
the day
at its completion,
uncompleted.

From The Court

I woke to someone shouting in the court.
I woke to the smell of gas: everyone was dead, myself included.

I woke to the outbreak of war and my clothes on fire.
It was quite still. Only father snored his reassuring snore.

I woke to so many catastrophes.
It was a training for the future.

At Forty-six

At forty-six, more than halfway
even long familiar voices may grow strange
like ice in June,
like things said or seen, and wounds
more difficult to heal.
Hard is the light that casts shadows
on that which is already in shadow,
and whatever grows
grows down into the earth, headfirst.
There is nothing but the children's voices,
the calls of migrating birds.

Picture

I was born, placed in a room
with windows, open,

the blind white,
the air as after rain,

spoke, now a child,
now grown-up

mourned for the dead,
loved those who were alive,

alone.

The Dream

This was how you looked at me in the dream.
There were others present, we were having coffee.
From an adjoining room light flowed
into the dark sense: I am dreaming.

You sat with your dark hair combed back.
Your mouth calm, your eyes restless, your wrinkles: close.
As though I had not seen you earlier
I turned to my maternal uncle
who was talking to someone on my left.
'But surely she's dead?' I said.
He stopped talking and turned towards me:
'Didn't you know?'

In the North

I have no dizzying view over valley and mountain.
The few flowers there are bloom late, and the grass
is patchy, thrusting its way laboriously up through clayey soil.
The beauty there in the south I accept and pass on
like a wondrous object that is almost without weight.
Here the abyss falls quite imperceptibly,
straight through grey days, small landscapes' mist.
Sometimes I'm seized with vertigo at quite low altitudes
as in a film starring the Harold Lloyd of fear:
the perspective's everything, particularly what it excludes.
What one doesn't see sharpens the eye and the emotions
and most rowanberries are both beautiful and bitter.

Life Was Given Me

Life was given me one morning of blizzards.
Cloths and bundles were snatched from the hands of the poor.
Out at sea there was no horizon.

Gramophones that brought a scent of foreign cities
blared Patti and the Charleston with a noise like sewing needles.
Sheet-metal roofing expanded with fright and burst,

out welled threadbare bonnets, rattan perambulators,
cut by rattling tramcars,
and the high-up misted windows gathered snow.

Life was given me where others shed it from themselves,
bodies no one saw merely sensed in the darkness.
Those dead folk: they knew everything about the living,

but the living knew nothing about the dead.

The Source

From a distance, over the fields
faintly but clearly
the springtime source can be heard.
I listen,
seek to get nearer.

Through the fresh,
sun-scented summer woods
the water echoes, ringing.
I go in my direction,
seeking.

Already amidst
the autumnal treetops
flickers the glen
where the concealed
beck purls.
I must rest.

As if there were snow in the air,
as if one's steps were infinite.
I listen, am near.
The voice from the source,
perpetually there,
invisible.

I Saw a Tree

I saw a tree
outside the tree,

it stood in its shadow
with dark top,

image imposed upon image,
its trunk rough,

like a scent, a cool freshness
in reality.

Walking through a Cool, Tall Forest

Walking through a cool, tall forest. Between the tree trunks
light from a deep clear valley with flowing water
that hurries ice-cold around your wrist, there in its glistening
        furrow.

Continuing towards the hills and taking the road back down to
        the house.
The mountain hawk's shadow barely perceptible above the grass
        in the wind.
Alone! But now a denser twilight in the forest,

now a longing for human voices and valleys.

Someone Has Gone out of the Room

Someone has gone out of the room
and left their clothes behind.
What is happening?

Someone couldn't manage to shut the door.
What was carried was heavy,
like the sofa, the table, or the bed.

Now everything is back in place, I think.
And the air will be fresher
when the window has been opened.

Now the wall can be painted over
so no stains are visible.
But the dampness still hangs in the air.

Someone has gone out into the sun,
can hardly be seen any more.

Whenever You Drive Up

Whenever you drive up to the 96 octane pump
there is always another car there, dirty, empty,
just standing there, the owner God knows where.
His plates show he's from the district.
At the self-service pump: no one.
Dirt and cold, neon lights even here,
and a deafening pneumatic drill
digging a hole for a new storage tank.

At the same time as you collect your bill you can buy
nougat, cassettes, porn mags, contraceptives
and with a full tank, your oil changed and your windscreen clear
drive out into the dark landscape
before a member of the gang that is hanging about outside
can pull at your car-door and, with a face
white as paper, staggering, shout something
you can't make out but which fills you with fear
or violent anger, later,
when you are alone on the road and the radio is playing
its wonderful, clear Vivaldi.

It Is Not Time That Alters Us

It is not time that alters us
but space: the forest that lay low like a dark band
around the evening when we were children.
And the water that came up to our feet.

It is the road that has been straightened out,
the trees, the houses, the same people
looking out of windows
that are windows in space, not time.

The room for children, the room for lovers
where birds fly in and out,
the room for one who sleeps so lightly
death's breathing cannot be heard.

The same furniture stands in the room,
the same branches outside it
as if it were your eyes' gaze,
that never ends.

Happiness

It felt as though all my life I had lived in a dark wood, and had
only now, for the first time, emerged from it. I stood facing a
large field that stretched down towards a quiet river.

I knew that someone was still standing in the shadow of the
wood, watching me, possibly intending to kill me. But the
morning was clear, every tree stood still. I thought: 'If this is all
they want of me, why don't I give it them? I've seen the field,
the river, the trees. Isn't that enough? This irksome life in the
wood, can't I be free of it? If not, why is this large field
stretching before me, why are the river, the trees so still? And
the dawn that is cool and pale, and the high spring sky, what is
the meaning of those? Have I not fulfilled my commitments?'

Slowly I walked through the tall, wet grass; cornflowers grew
there, glowing like precious stones, and in the air, which was

becoming ever warmer, there was a yellow cornfield that reached up to my shoulders. I walked in the direction of the faint singing down by the river. There I stopped. There was my wife, her breath white in the cold morning light, the trees aflame now, as though it were autumn. And the river water, which was almost black, mirroring the banks. How warm she is, how close to each other we are, as we watch the placid cows lying in the meadow, as heavy as clouds. That is why we are here, to see and feel, to help and support. The dark wood is only a backdrop, a dark border.

Hölderlin

1

The waggons roll
thundering in,
the weathervane chirrs
in the wind,
the torches are lowered
towards the eddies of the flood.
A face
shadowed by moonlight
is seen in the window of the tower
with a god's mask
wordlessly crying
like the child
in the mild autumn.

2

Once upon a time the poet sang
                    nature
    a life-giving potion, but now?
Icy and dead
or with tenderness not yet awoken
    the earth
that you must go under
    thrust your hands

like a hawthorn thicket
  towards the heavenly light
a sign

hurry then
  the breakwater stands mighty
but the sunken sea
  and no one
                is flung by waves
and over cities
              silence and
                      the wailing of stones

  3

'Familiar the shadows of the forests'
tracks in the snow a sign.

And the one who wakes in the mornings
by untrodden roads
sees above the ocean of the forests
the quiet of the boundless expanses
but also the dead who are there.

Sign and image
from this preserve
those who live in the eye.
Thus are restored
forest, road and springtimes to come.

CLAES ANDERSSON

(people, cracks)

The people, can you see them?
can you see them floating
down there in the underworld
can you see them drowning
up there among the TV antennae
can you see them deep within the fog that is
poisonous and yellow as death
can you see them taking wing
how they have been torn free
how their moorings have snapped
can you see them floating southwards
above the overgrown landscape
the resigned, abandoned houses
southwards
to the new cathedrals
of emptiness and slavery, can
you see them?
The people floating out
and away
across the waters, to countries that are
like the cries of strange creatures
incomprehensible and threatening
as epilepsy
can you see the great flocks
that are borne away by a wind that is stronger
than their will, people
like autumn leaves
like swallows on their way into
the great nests
stretched above the hungry continents
can you see their loneliness, their
lonely children
transfixed to the TV chair by a force
that is stronger than their will
can you see the children
who have long ago stopped crying
can you see them all, all those who have
long ago stopped caressing one another, all those
who are crushing one another with objects

heavy with melancholy
can you see them all those who are herded along
cooped up date-stamped clocked in
worn down used up, do you see
how sick many of them are, how
first they swell up
then shrink and are cleared away
to some ante-room storeroom
can you see them all
all those who sell their strength
their knowledge and their love
can you see how they are transformed
how something is transforming them
how their kisses are being transformed into bites
their tenderness into hunger
their warmth into ice
can you see the people
who are floating away from themselves, down
into the underworld
drowning up among the TV antennae
deep within the sooty clouds
can you hear the cries, the sobs
that are taller then the walls of the tower blocks
can you still hear them
before the poisonous yellow fog
eats away their outlines
and you find them choked
covered in slime
like fish
washed up on the loneliest of shores
the people, can you still see them?

from (after the depression)

What happens to be lit
is the visible
To write poems is to alter the lighting
so that the shadows, too, become distinct,
the treetops of the underworld...

Words that have not been lived conceal
Words that have not been lived through acquire vision
There someone is walking with a lantern through the dark
There in the darkness are all those
who are beginning to see but cannot yet be seen
Those who are concealed
It is them I want to write for

*

Don't idealise silence
Speech is gold
In silence grow rats and myxomatosis
Look at the tumour, how silently it eats you
There dialogue is superfluous
Don't imagine that the executioner sits chatting with his victims
Don't imagine that the tumour shouts good morning
Don't imagine that lovelessness owns up to its shortcomings
Don't imagine that bullets spend time wrangling
Do you suppose the rope is capable of tears?
Do you suppose sleeping pills sigh?
- Don't believe that anyone will write resolutions
if the rats have eaten his tongue out
Do you suppose barbed wire can be used as gramophone
        needles?
Don't imagine that anything grows in silence
except the silence to end all silences
All we think we are the masters of
masters us
Heaven water fire love
and death
We are mastered

*

There is a solitude that seldom leaves me in peace
The nights are drizzle and little children breathing
In a sense we grow younger as we grow older
and we learn the face's alphabet anew
learn to read the wrinkles round a mouth
and spell the furrows of a brow
What we keep silent about is what will not tolerate
the butchers' knives of words
We both know where we hid them
Solitude and silence are twins: not identical

but symbolic like sun and moon
To be born is to be expelled
We have not quite accepted the fact
That is why we are able to cope

from **(meetings, fragments)**

(to the memory of a girl)

She was small and bent and crooked
from TB of the spine as a child
Now she was nineteen
Whenever she lost her temper
she had one of her fits
She often fell in love
with the most self-assured boys
Then a light would go on in her face
The boys never paid any attention to her
Her lips would smile inwardly
as though she had a secret
no one else knew
or would ever share
One young lad who talked to himself
fell deeply and irrevocably
in love with her
She despised him
One evening when she was on her way home from the library
she was hit on the head and robbed
She was stricken mute and had one of her fits
A few days after that she fell asleep
and didn't wake up again

from (dreams, cement)

(for Medard Boss)

The sensual is not located in pictures
but in the beholder
Life is a projection
Two ladybirds copulate on a blade of grass
There's a swaying
A sucking in the pit of the stomach
High-frequency sounds have been discovered
which are capable of reducing us to idiocy
This may have already happened
But whenever on your travels you encounter a tree
think that it's the tree
which has encountered you
on its travels
Respect what exists
You are a part of it
That's a form of self-respect

(family life)

In the street a pregnant woman
toiling along with a perambulator
full of empty bottles
A few steps behind her
her staggering husband with
a screaming infant under one arm
Outside the liquor store she unloads the pram
and disappears inside
He puts the infant down in the pram
She comes out with a new bottle
which he roughly snatches from her hand
They return the same way they came
He leading the way and, after a moment's
hesitation, she following resolutely with the pram

Mumbles to himself the way lonely people do
Still has his longing. For whom? For what?
Laughs spastically when his desire to bite becomes too
    overpowering
Makes love with his eyes sewn-up
Thinks he has the body of a fish, gills, scales
Does his utmost half-heartedly
Fails in the essentials
Can live neither with nor without those he loves
Drags his body around with him to the most irrelevant places
Dreams about locomotives standing still, belching steam in the
    winter night. Snow
Seldom talks, seldom listens, pretends to listen while others are
    talking
Is scared of large dogs, attacks them in his sleep
Embarrassed by his privileges, conscience-addict
Omnipotently fancies that suffering alone grants the right to life
Obsessionally duty-conscious, at bottom asocial
Semi-autistic committee man, conference dreamer
Believes that all who think they are right are thereby mistaken
Unpretentious in a suffocating sort of way
Suspects most people are like him and is for that reason
    suspicious of them
Lies awake at night with his hand around his penis
Gets worked up about the wrong things at the wrong time in the
    wrong way
Secret monologues with Albert Schweitzer in secret rooms
Has been heard to say: 'comrades, don't fall asleep before
    you've taken your sleeping pills'
Occasionally trips and falls over, has visions, rejoices in the
    beauty of the earth
Thinks members of the RSPCA are cowards

(the new theology)

Illness is the body's conscience
What would we be without our illnesses
A lot of people marry them just to be
on the safe side
Some advertise: 'seek acquaintance with
discreet, balanced diabetes'

or:
'life-loving, well-situated lump seeks soft breast
Replies to undersigned. Yours eternally'
Paul Tillich tried to break down this symbiosis by means of group
        sex
Then death came and took him, but those were
interesting times, writes his 83-year-old widow
Checking one's blood pressure is also a kind of caress
Some people are just dying for someone to listen to their
        heartbeat
(the stethoscope leaves a wedding ring imprinted on their chests)
Older men prefer prostate massage
Certain young people slash their skin with razor-blades, their
        wounds
are screaming for love
Our illnesses stop us feeling lonely
We can depend on them as on lifelong friends
One can talk to one's illness
One can take it on holiday, to health resorts, sanatoria
It's as if one *had* it all the time
The neighbours don't start to gossip either
One can love it with at least half one's heart

(the love affair)

We collided, we fell through bedsheets of
light that made us invisible to each other, we
were hurled out of the frying pan into the embers. All that could
        have
become real in the frontier zone where growing and
withering clung to each other, all that united
us and set us beside ourselves
We knew it
We didn't know it
As usual, the truth was revealed in a dream:
splinters of glass through which our hands fumbled, the
        chainsaws

of our caressing hands, the bubbling
gas chambers of our capillaries, the congestion of our blood into
    erect stacks
Talked of that way it sounds menacing, but under the heaviest
    boulder
there was a disguised tenderness
We sat firmly belted into a driverless car that was moving at high
    speed
There was something in the road, we didn't see it
Something was hurled against the windshield and our faces
were smashed by the speed
The road was impassable, there was no road
And there it was an act of life took place with lights extinguished
During his lecture tour he noted down, inter alia, the following
    questions:
Does God exist?
What, in general, is it possible to express by means of words?
What is the meaning of entropy? (follow-up question) Is it
    dangerous?
Why do some people think they matter?
Is there any place for art in a socialist society?
Isn't the pronoun *man* ("one") simply an expression of
    misogyny?
If one really thinks about it, isn't it true that the mad are actually
    sane and vice versa?
Is it OK to experience grief? (follow-up question) Does it pass?
Why is one invariably disappointed whenever a writer opens
    his/her mouth?
Is form more important than form or whatever-it's-called?
What's the point of everything?
Is moral cowardice a typical Finnish weakness?
Have you ever seen that fellow Kihlman in the nude?
Why don't people like you go and live in Russia?
Why do people only write about gloomy things nowadays?
What is humour? (follow-up question) Well?
My wife says I have a violet aura, don't you think that's amusing?
Why do I always get rejected?
Is there a life after this one? (follow-up question) Or before this
    one?
What do you know about Gunnar Björling's homosexuality?

Eikö tämä ollutkaan suomenkielinen tilaisuus? *

Why shouldn't we have a drop of cognac of an evening if we're
    going to die soon?
Who asked you to come here, anyway (follow-up question) Who
    the hell asked you to come here, anyway?
Can one ever really succeed in saying anything definite about
    anything?
Isn't it time we started doing something instead of just sitting
    here talking?

* 'Oh, so you're not lecturing in Finnish?'

From The Last Summer of the Year

I could never have been a pathologist
I could never get used to the sweet-sour odour of opened
    cadavers
What business had I there, among those dead people?
If we'd met in life we wouldn't even have been on nodding
    acquaintance
What was there about their being dead that gave me the right to
    go cutting up their intestines?
The bodies of dead children filled me with anguish
I myself once came near to drowning when I was seven years old
I remember what it felt like to be dying – as though there weren't
    enough room
Later on I got to know (after a manner of speaking) several
    people who were brain-dead
Orgasm hasn't so much to do with death as people sometimes
    appear to believe
One always knows that one is going to come back
Autumn is a season of forgiveness, a kind of proxy
Once a year it dies for us, like Christ
Some therapists derive great satisfaction from looking after
    people who are dying, it makes them feel less lonely
Someone has said: 'It is necessary to get used to being dead'
I don't know, surely there are other things that are more
    important

Like getting used to life, for instance, and all those other people
I once knew a preparator at St Mary's Hospital
To watch him dissecting a corpse was like being present at a
    festive banquet
There were glasses and jars and vitrines which he fussed with and
    sipped from
He seemed to be able to get the best out of death: sentimen-
    tality and schadenfreude
I avoid going to the funerals of my friends and enemies
It's as if the friends were in the process of becoming slightly
    worse people
The enemies remain enemies however much they're dolled up
    with flowers and lies
Death is something I don't think about but have to stop myself
    thinking about all the time

I walk along Högbergsgatan
Hazy July sunshine, this uncertainty
Shouldn't I talk about it? The street
lies doubled up with blood in its gutter
The self-poisoning insects move jerkily
in their lanes. City folk in dark glasses
walk, their heads held high, like blind people
into this summer of uncertainty
A ragged woman plays the mouth-organ in the City Passage
Some tourists stone her with loose change which she
intercepts with a practised hand, in spite of her blindness
What are we doing? We are carrying plastic bags around, and all
    this
will tomorrow be turned to ashes, it has
already become altered
To recall what one felt without feeling it, like Fröding
The cloud pictures pitch around on the topsy-turvy square
Perhaps in a sense I am ill...
Or should I talk about the brief moments of numbness
When I awake towards morning and see
all the sleeping faces, Ville hugging his pillow
as though it were a lifebuoy in a water-filled cellar
A newspaper is whirling around in Esplanade Park, it looks like
a stray dog driven by hunger and curiosity
For a moment everything is new and unfamiliar, as it sometimes
    is

Poems in Our Absence

I

Your absence attracts me
I tremble for the moment when I may detect
submission in your eyes
I leave you constantly, so as to
remain. Having come thus far I know
that all attempts at flight are nothing
but a change of prison, the sudden, dizzying sensation
in our rushes between longings behind cage-bars
At every moment we are pursued, caught up with
and already lost, and the war of containment goes on
perpetually in the trenches of our skin, in every pore
of the concrete desert we inhabit. Like an intoxication, a swiftly
flaring dream was the moment we lived, in
the *statu nascendi* of disintegration and redemption
as we were abandoned and exposed for the sake of someone
            else, unknown

II

The long periods of absence. Where was I
during the daily roll-calls?
Absent. Away. And your absent body
like a shadow on the wallpaper of the hotel room
Was I in you that time? Did we meet?
No. I was absent: I scarcely
noticed the children clambering in and out of my embrace
as on some old oak tree standing withered and silent, a
wraith of the woods, paralysed in its grief-stricken
murmuring between root and crown
Not even in drunkenness did I come nearer myself, not even
in dreams did I become more visible to myself
My journey held too much of flight. But our shadows
coincided and imprisoned us, a shadow
of something that was past but drew tormentingly close
One day the eldest children stood like giant sun-
flowers looking down at me

'You've to wake up, Dad! You're needed!' Who? Who's
needed? Needed for what?
And as if it were a matter of course the child who once
had been the youngest, most beloved, took me in his arms
and I became a child again, present in his close
presence

III

It sometimes happens that, mortally wounded, we catch hold
of each other like hooks, the more severely gashed
the more eager in our attempts to free ourselves
We are growing old, hooked together, arm in arm
like some folk-dance couple from the Magic Lantern Era

IV

Life is deepest uncertainty, art is
deepest uncertainty, joy is deepest sorrow
Sorrow is deep trust, hope is self-
deception, deception is deepest honesty
Kisses bite, caresses precede strangling, strangling
fingers remember a kitten, the penis
is a barb, the vagina a ravine
Sincerity is sadism, nothing kills like
intimacy, nothing kills like distance, the orgasm
is radioactive, creation is improductivity
Where there is no room for bliss there is room for
the anguish out of which the poem is pressed into the paper

V

We often talk about togetherness, but we
experience it more and more rarely
When it occasionally happens we are seized
with panic. We flee
We often talk about the importance of talking, but
we only grow more mute, even as we utter our words
We become a part of our muteness and loneliness, we

need the protection they afford us
The muteness that possesses us makes room
for the voices of others
Desertion becomes the context of our lives, a
way of coping when we can't cope
Someone has come too close to us
We have left each other in rage

VI

He was so aggressive that one felt
like biting his cock off

VII

One can't own another person!
Say that one can't!
OK?
But one can love her, love
her until she no longer knows who she is, where
she has come from or where she was on her way to, whom
she left or why
One can love her, love
her until she no longer remembers who
once used to care for her, who it was wished her
well, whom she was important to, what dreams
she bore next to her heart
One can love her, love
her until she no longer remembers what she
wanted out of life
One can love her until she stops growing, until
she stops, quite simply, in the midst of everything!

VIII

As when one is sitting watching a film at the cinema
and the film suddenly breaks
and one can neither whistle nor stamp
because one is in some way paralysed

and because one doesn't know whether it is the film
or oneself that has become invisible, that was
what it felt like when you left me for someone else
Later when you came back I at first experienced
nothing, then an all-consuming joy, an
all-consuming hatred
Meanwhile someone had changed the film
What was now showing was a cruel and technically
sophisticated war between small children who had all
somehow grown together
I tried to jerk my hand free but noticed
that it was your hand, and that the person who was sitting
beside me was not you but myself.

Living Together Elegies

*But you! You don't mean
a word of what I say!*

I

Everything I did with you lacked intention
There is no such thing as intentional regret or intentional sorrow
There is no such thing as intentional hatred
But year after year the search for your face
filled me
It did not appear   It did not exist
It took up all my time
But in the meanwhile: so many knocked-down gazes
rejected smiles!
You got tired of my roving
You left me for someone else
I was forced to grow   Now I live alone with you
It hurts but otherwise everything is much better
There is no such thing as intentional hatred
One doesn't even have to think about it

G

II

I caught sight of you where Nostrilwing Path
crosses Mouthside Lane
It was something o'clock then too
I got caught in the little wrinkle that appeared
exactly where you smiled
An empty bed came rolling down the slope
All one had to do was jump into it and let oneself be carried away
In many respects it was a simple journey
We arrived at the sea as the sun was rising
Seagulls hung up to dry against the azure sky
There was the house of which we had dreamed
You were more enthusiastic than ever
Little children sprang up in the corners, with milk teeth
and plaintive cries
I had never lived in a nesting-box before
There was very little room
When winter came we chopped up the bed for firewood
That was possibly shortsighted
We had to sleep standing up
You couldn't agree with me about anything when we saw the
          family therapist
It's like the mushrooms and the sand
One never succeeds in getting rid of it entirely
Its scrunch between your teeth used to drive me insane

III

First you wouldn't promise anything
Then you fulfilled what you hadn't promised
Then you promised never to be unfaithful to me again
Then you were unfaithful to me (after all, you hadn't promised
          anything)
From the start I swore to be faithful to you
I was unfaithful to you
It had never got started
You were beside yourself
You regretted everything, promised anything
I've been unfaithful to you, I said, sincerely (in order to kill you)
You took back everything

You were unfaithful to me, definitively
I flew into a rage, tried to kill myself
I tried to be unfaithful to you
It was no longer possible
I was no longer I
I had become you
I couldn't be unfaithful to myself, in you
We lost everything we never cared about having
Thereby we lost everything

IV

Pulverised to tears and flour
Blackened to glue
Lashed our faces to shreds with white sticks
Got our sex organs mixed up
Unconcerned, happy in our mortal remains

V

Each morning I throw you up, my beloved
Your love is so nutritious it is starving me
I am burning like the cross you say you bear
for my sake
I long for the earth I can hold down

VI

I lay awake beside you and
was happy in the darkness
You were asleep   The ringdove on the metal window-sill
was asleep with its head under its wing
I didn't dream about a waterfall
inside the mountain
I dreamt I was a tree that
was felled from behind with an axe
I fell with my face to the mountain
The mountain shattered. Underneath it was
another mountain   It held

VII

If you leave me I will die
That point is not far off   And you know it
You know that we both know
Whose fault do you think it will have been?

Not yours alone, possibly?
You are all I have   That isn't much
But do as you will, if you have any will
You mustn't bother about me, you mustn't
obey me   That's an order!
Be something to yourself, take control of your life
Do what you will but don't forget what that entails
Don't say afterwards you weren't warned
It was all done for your sake, after all
I could easily have chosen someone else
Where would you have gone then
You really begged for it, in that loathsome way of yours
Is this all the thanks I get, all my reward
There won't be any flowers on my grave
At least promise me not to die before I do
You can at least spare me that disgrace
Go on, then, do it!

VIII

I'm a little busy right now
My head stuck in the lift door
I'm going up actually   See you?

IX

We saw so little of
all that was given us
There was so little we managed to hold on to
of all that was taken from us
Where was Joy off to – she that most often arrived
uninvited, followed by her sister Anguish
in her dress made of bandage cloth?

Who killed the sexuality? Buried
in a wrinkle?
Yet still! The rare moments
of presence! The tropical birds! Kingfishers!
Golden orioles! Bee-eaters! Beautiful, transient creatures
scarcely brushing our skins, scarcely tasted
by our blood before they were gone once more
plunged into the same depths from which they had been hurled

X

You laugh through me
as I fall
through your laughing face I see
your weeping face
Immediately underneath, a face twisted
with rage
Behind them the remnants of a smile
And beneath them all, like a hint, the astonished
face of a small child
Through them all stares a death mask
It stares through me from your
distorted, partially disintegrated faces

XI

Maybe it would be nice to feel your cock
in my cunt, but partly I find you repulsive and partly
you attract me so violently that I can feel
nothing but loathing at such a strong desire
It is obscene
If I refuse to fuck with you
you will linger in me
You will remain in me
If I fuck with you you will leave me
as soon as I have washed myself off
I shall choose a third way, I shall stop seeing you!
You're going into a kind of breakdown
You're behaving strangely
I don't recognise you

Now I'll be able to visit you in peace and quiet
in the ward, the rest will be hidden
inside me, growing there, blessed

XII

What we remember are, of course, the losses
and the late-found sense of presence
Why did we not experience it?
What kind of a postmortem is that?
We used words without their contents, like
gutted bodies
Our speech was turned to a cipher
of denials and the denials of denials, until
the words formed like a crust of ice around our lips
All the understanding? All we wanted?
Our meetings were like the embraces of dried flowers
in absolute silence
And we used to speak of them as 'storms'!
We took self-contempt in homeopathic doses
Like those food additives that are supposed to guarantee
eternal youth
Death laid its siege
We endured it with a tired grimace torn
from one of our worn-out faces

XIII

Blackbird morning   Wind from the lilac bushes
Shoulders of cumulus clouds that the sun borders with gold
You come in with the light's corridor in the nape of your neck
Your hips enclose an exact science
My shadow is disturbed and is merged
with yours, which deepens
We move jerkily like waterfleas
on the surface of desire
Total abandonment may only exist
in memory, says Olof Lagercrantz

XIV

Nowadays I trust you as little
as I have always trusted myself
As soon as I turn my back you are unfaithful to me
You're right to do it
That is what I would do if I were myself
In a way I am no longer myself
I'm subject to long attacks of faithfulness and devotion
It's a form of revenge
Now when there's nothing left to massacre
we could have a reasonable life together you and I
But you! You don't mean a word of what I say!
Go to hell but don't come back again

XV

We are lying naked on our backs beside each other
We have just made love
Saturday morning   The window is knocking gently in the May
        wind
The birch trees are glowing faintly
The old transistor radio is playing two
programmes at the same time: Ravel's F major String Quartet
        and, as if
from the other side of a great field, a
talk on crop rotation
We lie in silence, listening, your left hand
on my shoulder, my hand cupped
around one of your breasts
You are cool, impassive
Soon the children will be here, before they vanish

XVI

I wish I were you
at the moment you are being unfaithful to me
I wish I were your lover
at the moment he remembers me

I wish you were I
at the moment you come back
I wish myself free of your membranes
They are stamping me black

XVII

Something is drying withering shrivelling
losing its leaves and eyes and fingers
But the root is floating about under the ground
with its blind unhappy eyes

From About My Future Life as a Garden Lawn

Andersson what an infernal noise
Andersson can't even stand up straight
Andersson isn't going to turn into anything much
Andersson is a coward
Andersson damn well ought to pull himself together before it's
     too bloody late
Andersson is shaking like an aspic jelly
Andersson drinks too much
Andersson shouldn't smoke in his sleep
Andersson isn't really there for a good part of the year
Andersson ought to start putting his house in order
Andersson shouldn't be going to Mallorca right now when his
     old mother is lying here at her last gasp
Andersson eats like a pig or a piglet
Andersson is fat
Andersson ought to take up the clarinet instead
Andersson shouldn't imagine he has rights he hasn't got
Andersson ought to take his finger out
Andersson ought to join the union instead of sitting there
     shooting his fucking mouth off
Andersson should realise that he ought to look after his own
     personal hygiene as much for his own sake as for anyone
     else's

Andersson isn't much of a Christmas present
Andersson ought to realise that Andersson isn't only
    Andersson's own private concern
Andersson ought to see that he can't just lie there like a corpse
    all day having a good time
Andersson has been getting too big for his boots lately to be
    quite honest
Andersson must stop squinting
Andersson shouldn't come and complain after the event that
    Andersson wasn't informed in time about Andersson's
    situation
Andersson has got to stop whistling, or bloody else
Andersson must not forget to take his medicine or Andersson is
    going to die and that will be that
Andersson where the hell is Andersson
Andersson can't have
Andersson shouldn't have jumped that's what I say to be
    perfectly honest
Andersson might at least have closed the window after him

From Here Begins All That Remains

June the thirteenth   Light of summer
    psalms, the same greenness as in memory, a
mite diluted by their prognoses
    I listen to the weather report from
coastal stations, try to imagine the weather
    in places familiar and unfamiliar
while the voice of Sinbad booms like a
    bellbuoy over the radiowaves: Clear!
Clear! Clear? I cycle along the shore
    in towards the city centre flooded through by
holy air, my soul is a deathshead
    moth fluttering from cairn
to cairn   All the unthinkable! It's
    itching, and 'to become a person is to become
a conversation'   In the shopping mall the blind
    grope their way among the electronic

eyes, the automobiles coagulate in my veins, a cold
    draught comes through the windshields of my eyes
I watch the homeless wandering monks
    on their pilgrimage from trashcan to trashcan
What is my share in their homelessness?
    Last night I dreamed I
put on my confirmation suit
    and cycled to the maternity hospital, where
a party was underway, all the brides were
    eighty that day   They had run out of children
Submerged in my diver's bell I note down
    everything in approximately the order
it disappears in   A certain
    denial   A certain splitting-off   A
certain preoccupation   Yet the greenness
    is almost the same   Can one go on
living like this, without regret?

GÖSTA ÅGREN

Enlargement

Fear stops, the
body's extra heart,
which nevertheless does not help.
It is impossible
to prolong life; let
us enlarge it
with simplicity. This
is merely the poem's
attempt to say everything
by not doing so.

Prehistory

The voices are there, but
they are as yet empty.
As yet no words are needed.
As yet no one has anything
to hide.

The Meaning

He said: we are cells
in God's brain. The body
is merely a pause, which
must be overcome. And
he said: this wandering
is an idea. This treachery,
all starved violence, all
powerful hunger, constitutes the goal. For
the goal of a journey is not
that which is attained, but all
that we leave behind. The great
civilisation we build

up, God's brain, is
meaningless. The meaning
is the darkness we
fight. I did not
believe him.

Treachery

Dante sent the foe
against Florence. One
can betray only
that which one loves. Treach-
ery is the fire
that keeps loyalty
warm. Friendship is the
knife one refrains
from using. The foe
is not he that takes
Florence, but he
that does not care
to take it.

Shore

Here, on the shore's deadened
rocks, this immense
afternoon of stone,
a solitary fledgling teeters
along through the sudden
dream that is called life.
In every miracle there is
pain. Even stone
has its single, slow
pulsebeat. It is only the sea's
change that never
changes. Searching

you go, and continue
to go. Already the sand is
filled with writing. You wander
in your own footprints. You are
one of your own followers. But
the tide of time rises at last,
lingering, a sigh of water
rises, welling
in across the shore

Genetic

The upper classes protect themselves
against the people with
intelligence tests. So the children of the people
must be taught stupidity,
before they are tested.
That takes many years. The
clever ones learn it in the
end, but the stupid ones
never do.

Courage

He that lacks courage
does not dare to be afraid.
Only he that dares
to meet fear dares to meet
danger. He is the one who
lets his pain well forth
and so transforms it
into sorrow, that season
without suffering. He dares
to live. Death is for
him only a part
of his funeral.

Epitaph by the Shore at Vasa

Here lie the shadows
that are cast by a few
drink-destroyed lives. They
know that man
is good. He caresses
the beast of slaughter. Everything is
put to use, even death. Of it
there remains nothing
but to die. Their
feelings have slackened
to memories. Their
souls are one out of many
viscera. Not to smile
through tears and simply
say how one is suffering
may be the only way
of doing so. The summer night
grows shimmeringly dark.
The police car stops.

And Thereby

In the midst of the greenness
one sees red, wide-
open cries. This form
of pain is called roses.
Waiting is a darkness
in which all that is to happen
is still to come, but living
is the painful fire
of strength that consumes
our lives, and thereby
gives them meaning.

The Immobile

The immobile is like
an intention. We can
prevent a journey, but
who can stop
the one who is waiting?

Birds of Passage

They come. Each
generation yearns upwards
to their yearning.
When autumn draws nigh
the birds return deathwards
as though that were their goal.

A National Minority

This silence is
my people. Still
we exist, still our flight
persists. For some the goal
is power, that hiding-place
for weakness. He that is silent
about oppression likes to do it
in speeches; words are more silent
than silence. But the others
travel away in order to become
foreigners. They leave
themselves at home; borne upright
by liquor their bodies travel
alone towards their new souls. The
rest of us do not travel away, this too
a journey, but longer. We

remain here, we speak
our language. So distinct
is life.

Summary

All his life
he sought in vain
for a way to live his life. That
was the way.

The Prisoner

My crimes have been
committed, my cell is locked
I am free.

And Then

And finally he came to
reality. He grew afraid
of his courage, for here
there was no possibility
of defence. He was
his own body. And knowledge
proved to be his own
ignorance, but clearer
and greater. It embraced
atoms and galaxies, but not
reality, that place
in the soul. All he finally
found was goodness, a kind
of residence in knowledge, and then
stayed put in the dark,
bleeding ranks.

Life and Poetry

It is quiet. A runnel
of seconds trickles from
the overfull clock.
The brain has intensified to
fire. The heart butts
its blood through
the veins. To write
poems is to touch
oneself in order to see
if one is still alive.

Life and Tears

Weeping is
the weak's way of
living.
Living is
the strong's way of
weeping.

Majniemi

The heavy eternity
of museums is not
here. If the room
lacks walls one can never
escape from it. The limitless
universe is a trap.
But here the wind passes through
the trembling tears of
the weeping birch. Here the cabin
still creeps forward in its low passage
of time. Eternity has not

yet reached here, here
it merely exists.

Majniemi: the summer cottage of Zachris Topelius
in the archipelago of Nykarleby, now a museum.

Ego

The person who never changes
becomes another.

Black and White

Reality is bloody
with content, but it lacks
form. Thus art is
neither feelings nor
thoughts. It is structure, an
attempt to control
feelings and thoughts. For it may even
be a method of opposing
content. The front line of
our civilisation
passes through slim volumes.
The Gesamtkunstwerk of
death and hunger in which
we live can be transfigured only
by the sternness that is called
form. It is
in the black-and-white movie
that colours blaze. Form is
restriction. The artist
shuts himself in
in order to be free.

Lyric Poetry

While the spring aches
in the snow like a poem
in the silence, and no one
can see the fire that rages
white where the water
beats against the cliff, and
the leaves, at last strong
with weariness, manage to
free themselves and sink
into the cadence whose in-
visible pillars have always
supported them, we speak
from this shore without
sea that is called body,
constantly pierced through
by spears of blood from
the heart, protected only
by its existence, and all
we can say is
this.

Identity

Hamlet plays crazy
because he is.
By being someone
else the spy is
himself. His identity
consists in being
absent. Even the actor
is merely one
of his roles. They
migrate from person
to person. Slowly, from this,
humanity is formed.
Just now I am writing
with this hand.

The Fifth of July

We no longer love
our love for our native land.
Our love is the face
of hatred. Life still goes on
in this darkness that is called
body, but we lack an
immortal soul, and so our lives
are worthless.
We can no longer afford
to sacrifice them. The earth
is merely a blue island
in eternity. We only dare
to love the limit-
less: native place and mother tongue,
the only place that exists
everywhere, the only language
everyone speaks.

Summer Vigil

An incandescent lung
in the north waits for
the sun's cigarette. Your
sleeping face resembles
a message. But who
is sending it? Long we have
walked side by side
in the deepening alley of the years.
The gravel thickens to darkness
at last, but the face of
a man is clearer than
his thoughts, his name
deeper than the darkness
of feelings in which
he is locked. Now
night hardens to day.
Now your sleep is all the twilight
that is left.

The Price

To have once been
able to fly is
the price every
bird must pay
for once having been able
to fly.

God

God is physical. These
roads are the nerves
on his heart. Sil-
ence is what he looks like.
On his human organ
he plays the scale
that spans fear and space.
Nothing is anything
else. In every newborn infant
beats a secret god. In
every tree a finger points
earthward. Friend, it is only the
soul that dies. The body
is eternal.

There

There is a bottom
to everything. There weariness
grows weary, and wounds
grow numb. There torments
darken, there of love
remains only
the heart, and of faith

only the deed. Weakness is there
the strength that can never
fail. There the future
is robbed of
all its hurt.

Interlude

Can I make the words go
deeper with me? The last
page is always white
with silence, but which
will be this last white page,
where the words disappear
in the paper's pale
moonlight? The goal consists
not in the intense
silence, hearing's inner,
streaming rain, but in
the silence in whose cloud
the words slowly die until
only the poem is left.

Gerd Ågren
(a retarded child)

She looks at her body. There
is no soul that can cast
this shadow. Her life
will never be reduced
to a loftier meaning. Strong
as the heart she is
she leads her pulse against the
darkness of the waiting wall.
Life is the only phase
in her life. She caresses

intensely; entrusts her
hands to your body. If life is
meaningless, it must be
a gift.

The Starving, Too

The starving, too, can
love, but their love is
simplified to hunger, its
principle. With the help of
another's love the sated love
themselves, which they
otherwise would hate. And
stronger is perhaps the love
that saves,
but deeper is the one
that seals. People, of
whom all that is left is
a heart and its
two arms, give one another
their hunger.

In a Glade

Whoever simplifies his life
to art evades it. Our
desperate scrawling on the wall
cannot hide it. Nonetheless
I write once more: Here is
the source, waiting like hunger.
Here is the church window of the spruce-fir
onto the dark. Here the path's
searching shadow dies in the grass.

The Hunter

The beast crouches. Cloudy
and grey, its brain waits for
blood. A restless wound
in the skin of stillness
draws ever nearer. The beast of
prey tautens to pounding
darkness. The hare stops,
the trees stop, the shot
detonates. The hunter gets up,
human once more. Only
the action frees wholly
from the action. And yet
he is silent. The crime
can be expiated, but never
the resolve.

R. S. Thomas

In vain he looks up
at the deadly silent hunger
that is called space; patient-
ly he contemplates
the buds of spring: they open,
sudden cries that congeal
to flowers. It is a matter
of waiting. In November
he goes over to
the window. Yes, the landscape
is visible again. The summer
was only its transient
body.

Anna Akhmatova

St Petersburg; the light footsteps
draw near. The houses are hazy
with time, but everything that happens
has the clarity of ritual
in this city, the shore
of infinite Russia.
In reality it is 1940
and the rattling waves of the sea
the inaudible future of the steppe
are drowning in cries and prayers.
To remember is resignation;
it is to choose one's own
defeat, a clear
victory. Not to surrender, but
to stand still. It is masquerade
time in St Petersburg. The dance glides on
and reality waits, the
lonely woman. It is war,
she writes.

Waking

Inside sleep he heard
the wave of footsteps moving towards him
over the sea of the floor. Eyes looked
at his brain. The voice
fumbled like a hand. Waking
was a way of
not answering. He looked up.
Slowly his gaze was veiled
by consciousness.

But

To have reached the goal
demands perseverance.

Copernicus

Someone looked for the first time
out towards the emptiness, shielded
only by his face. And
of his lost faith he missed
most the freedom
doubt had given.

Spring

Through the sparse movements
that surround its nest, the bird
stares at eternity. Its eye
is wide-open and void. But
softly the cloudy birdbreast
sinks down, and
wells like hot mist over
the blind eggs.

The Spruce-Firs

Spruce-firs do not
exist. The earth
is probing with dull
fir-needle searchlights
in the opaque
light.

Step One

They seek certainty
and darkness, not
knowledge. The answer is
the stone that kills
the bird of enigma.

Return

He drifts without will in
the foetal waters of sleep.
And he awakes, saved
from his depths. Somewhere
farthest down in sleep
something is waiting.

Diagnosis

The traveller attempts to travel
to the horizon. And
the hunter attempts to shoot
happiness. They demand
what is, in place of
what always is.

The Mother

Fearfully they looked at the silence
in her tautening face.
What did she demand of them? Goodness
and wisdom? The children ran
out to play. All
they could give her was
cruelty and love.

Momentary image

The padding dog
embroiders his spiralling
threadwork on the meadow's white
tablecloth, and vanishes. So
one should always go:
cautiously, as though it were a matter of
touching a brain;
distinctly, as though it were a matter of
describing a walk;
calmly, as though there lurked
a danger.

Europa

Sudden as a short-cut was
love. Now a veil of tears
conceals the bare kitchen. Now
she listens alone, in the rain
from the ticking clock,
and the airliner flies through
the night and the cities drift
southward like misty flowers.

Alas. A farewell is never
over. Love is immortal.
Farewell, but forever. The
gaping wounds in the pictures:
death riding over the squares
clad in metal; the forests of ruins
– all this culture is only a face
concealing the soul of Europe,
that old, tear-filled song.

The Cathedrals of Europe

They are the immense radio sets of
the medieval era, tuned
to a single station, which transmits
silence without a break.
The message is that there is
a message; something so simple
words cannot explain. Cathedrals
are needed. But
wave follows upon wave; strength
grows into fatigue. Like a
trackless heath the 13th century's
human mass stands beneath the sky.
Now our knowledge is greater,
but also our ignorance. The

stronger reality becomes,
the deeper is its shadow.
The pillars stand like longing
waists; hymns of light
stream in through the windows.
Night falls, eyes
grow dim, stars
burn.

Bird

True birds
can fly, and therefore have
no need of doing so.
They even lack wings.

In the North

What is it that protects the earth
so that the permafrost cannot penetrate
any deeper?
You know the answer: the permafrost.

In Ostrobothnia

Here each town is a
footnote to the forest's
melancholy mass of text,
here the horizon bares
its teeth. Here freedom shrinks

to restlessness. Here necessity grows
into tranquillity. One travels away
in an attempt to prevent
what must happen. One stays
here, and as the years go by
life grows simplified until
there are left only earth
and sky.

Circle

All is as before. The clock
glows in the morning darkness. But
every answer diminishes the question,
every legend must be told
at last. You have moved
in your sparse constellation
of years; you have waited.
Nothing is as before, for
nothing has happened. You never dared
to receive, and your gifts
were only a protective wall.
It is growing light; in the east
red organ music is rising. My friend,
you have misunderstood everything.
Life is not the goods, it is
the price. Empty-handed you turn round,
but it doesn't matter. Everything
is as before; soon
you will be home again.